# Flipping Your Englis
# to Reach All Learne

Learn how flipping your English language arts classroom can help you reach students of different abilities, improve classroom management, and give you more time to interact with each student. This practical book shows why Flipped Classrooms are effective and how they work. You will discover how to flip your instruction in writing, reading, language, and speaking and listening while meeting the Common Core State Standards. A variety of step-by-step lesson plans is provided.

**Troy Cockrum** is a middle school language arts teacher from Indiana. He is also a Google Certified Teacher and host of the Flipped Learning Network Podcast.

## Other Eye on Education Books Available from Routledge (www.routledge.com/eyeoneducation)

# Flipping Your English Class to Reach All Learners

## Strategies and Lesson Plans

Troy Cockrum

Routledge
Taylor & Francis Group

NEW YORK AND LONDON

First published 2014
by Routledge
711 Third Avenue, New York, NY 10017

And by Routledge
2 Park Square, Milton Park, Abingdon, Oxon OX14 4RN

*Routledge is an imprint of the Taylor & Francis Group, an informa business*

*Library of Congress Cataloging-in-Publication Data*

Cockrum, Troy.
Flipping your English class to reach all learners : strategies and lesson plans /
  Troy Cockrum.
    pages cm
  Includes bibliographical references and index.
  1. Language arts (Elementary)—Study and teaching—United States.
  2. Language arts (Elementary)—Standards—United States.  I. Title.
  LB1576.C5675 2014
  372.6—dc23
  2013037753

ISBN: 978-0-415-73468-4 (hbk)
ISBN: 978-0-415-73315-1 (pbk)
ISBN: 97801-315-81982-2 (ebk)

Typeset in Bembo
by Apex CoVantage, LLC

Printed and bound in the United States of America by Publishers Graphics, LLC on sustainably sourced paper.

# Contents

# Meet the Author

**Troy Cockrum** is a middle school language arts teacher in Indianapolis, Indiana. He does training and consulting across the country specializing in incorporating technology into the classroom, especially through Google Apps for Education and Flipped Learning. He became a Google Certified Teacher in 2011. In addition, he is a member of the Flipped Learning Network Cadre, a small network of educators endorsed by the Flipped Learning Network to train and present on Flipped Learning, and he also hosts the Flipped Learning Network Podcast. In 2013, he was named a Jacobs Educator Award recipient by the Indiana University School of Education.

Prior to becoming an educator, Troy was a television writer/producer and earned a regional Emmy nomination in 2002. In his spare time, he coaches soccer and performs improv comedy. He would like to someday be on the television show *Survivor.*

# Acknowledgments

I would like to thank Debra Heimbrock and Pam Pendry for encouraging me to be a better educator and risk taker. I was blessed to have both of you as my mentors when I was launching my teaching career. A special thanks goes to Kate Baker, Amie Trahan, April Gudenrath, Ric Reyes, and Kate Petty for proofreading, advising, and challenging my thinking. I thank Jerry Flynn for allowing me the freedom to explore innovative ideas in my classroom. I thank Jon Bergmann and Aaron Sams for being so open and willing to share their ideas and encouragement and Ramsey Musallam for continuously challenging me to reflect on my own teaching and my students' learning. I've also been blessed to have so many wonderful students and coworkers, too many to name here.

Finally, I want to thank my mom and dad for all their support throughout my life.

# Why I Flipped My Class

I was distraught. I had found myself in that troublesome spot where many other teachers—maybe even you—have been before. I was just into my fourth year of teaching and was on the verge of quitting the profession. I was teaching middle school language arts and felt like I spent endless hours grading papers, managing classroom behavior and staff meetings, and trying to find ways to encourage students to meet certain standardized expectations. I realized these various tasks are part of a teaching career. The issue wasn't so much that I minded doing them. It was more problematic that I wasn't seeing the learning results. I wasn't seeing my students achieve those "Aha!" moments we teachers so tirelessly work to get. I was passionate about student learning and it seemed I spent more time focused on student accountability.

I continually asked myself the question, "What is the best use of my class time with my students?" I knew individualized instruction was essential for quality learning. But how could I achieve that with 25 or more students in a class? I knew that being able to guide students' specific questions while they were working on an assignment was important to their success. But how could I be available to all my students when they were working and creating? Many teachers, having 50–150 students or more, even if they made themselves available via e-mail, could spend hours of their personal time answering all their students' questions. I knew that I wanted my students to do more high-order thinking and to be creative. I wanted to teach problem solving, critical thinking, and collaboration, but how could I find the time? How could I challenge the higher-achieving students to go deeper without at the same time ignoring or discouraging the lower-achieving students? How could I support students at their pace while still meeting all the standards the teaching field required? How could I encourage students to guide their own learning when I had so many of them to assess for standards? In short, how could I create a personalized learning environment for each student so that all of the students could grow and develop to the best of their ability? All these questions were answered, to my surprise, by the Flipped Classroom.

Now, I'll be honest. The first question I had hoped to answer with Flipped Learning was: how could I gain more class time to cover the material I needed to cover? That is what originally drew me to Flipped Learning. Answering all these questions kept me using Flipped Learning and brought me to where I am today, which will probably not be the same place six months from now. Flipped Learning is a process that consistently improves you and allows you to do things in your class you never had time for before. It's like a spouse who constantly demands you be a better person. Flipped Learning constantly demands you be a better teacher.

Let me back up a little. My journey into Flipped Learning started before I made the actual decision to flip my class. Prior to 2010, I had been gradually introducing more technology to my classroom. One piece this year, another piece the next. It was a very hodgepodge approach with little consistency. I'd hear about a great Web site or online tool and jump on it. I didn't put a lot of thought into how technology supported learning; I was just enamored with the tool. Then, I decided one of my strengths as a teacher could be my ability to infuse the curriculum with technology in an organized, meaningful way. I worked formerly in the mass media industry and was required to continually learn and be on the cutting edge of technology. I was stupefied to come into the classroom and see such an aversion to technology in a lot of areas of education, from the classroom to professional development. Whether it be because of fear or budgets, technology was not at the forefront for a lot of education professionals. I decided to take the leap to more technology by cannon balling in and stopping the piecemeal, disorganized way I had utilized it in the past. However, you don't need to be particularly innovative in your use of technology to flip your class; you just need to be willing to step out of your comfort zone and learn. As with any teaching method, reflection of practice is a key component for a successful flipped class.

I already used the Writing Workshop model (discussed more in Chapter 4). I started using that in 2008 because I saw the value of working with students in the classroom. But it wasn't quite meeting all my needs. Then I read *The Digital Writing Workshop* by Troy Hicks and got inspired to forge forward (2009). In November of that year, I attended the NCTE convention in Orlando for the first time. One of the biggest highlights happened on day one when I saw Troy Hicks, Bud Hunt, and Sarah Kajder present a session titled *Creating Opportunities for Learning with Newer Literacies and Technologies: Three Reports from Cyberspace* (2010). Hearing these speakers not only gave me great ideas and inspiration to bring into my classroom, it also validated my decisions on the uses of technology and the importance of building twenty-first-century skills with my students. If you're reading this book, you probably agree.

Later during that conference, I stumbled into a session called *Using Google in Ways That Haven't Even Been Invented Yet: Visionary Reports from Cyberspace*

(Zellner & Beauchamp-Hicks, 2009). In this session, I watched Andrea Zellner, Sara Beauchamp-Hicks, and, again, Troy Hicks talk about their uses of Google Apps™ for Education. I sat in that session seeing small snippets of what these teachers could do and said to myself, "I want to do that." Their presentation inspired me to not only use Google in my class a lot more, it also inspired me to attempt to become a Google Certified Teacher. I was fortunate to be accepted into the Google Teacher Academy a year and a half later. It probably seems like I'm rambling here. "What does this have to do with flipping?" you may be asking. Well, I bring up my Google experiences because that is when I first met Ramsey Musallam, who has greatly influenced my views on how my Flipped Classroom currently operates.

As my teaching and technology infusion progressed, I came across the concept known as the Flipped Classroom sometime in December 2010. I saw a video made by TechSmith on YouTube™ (http://www.youtube/2H4RkudFzlc) of Aaron Sams talking about his Flipped Classroom. A friend of mine who taught middle school math had been looking for ways to differentiate his classroom, and I passed this video on to him as a suggestion. He got very excited about trying it for a variety of reasons and began asking me questions since he believed the model sounded very similar to what I was already doing. It was at some point during those discussions, and after subsequent research, that I realized I could blend the flipped model with the workshop model and buy myself more in-class work time while still delivering the necessary content that would have been in the mini-lessons. And that was the birth of my foray into Flipped Learning.

As I researched more during that semester, I followed the Flipped Classroom Ning (flippedlearning.org), and came across the Flipped Classroom Conference (now known as FlipCon) in Woodland Park, Colorado put on by Jon Bergmann and Aaron Sams. On a whim, not really expecting to get it approved, I showed it to my principal (including all associated costs), and to my surprise he said, "Sounds great. Go for it!"

Attending the conference was the best decision I could have made because when I decided to go, I still wasn't fully sure I wanted to flip. I absorbed so much information from Jon Bergmann, Aaron Sams, Brian Bennett, April Gudenrath, Jason Kern, and several others at the conference. I saw the passion these educators brought to their classrooms. I saw the nuts and bolts of making it work. It brought a great deal of clarity and confidence to the potential of this model.

At the time, I hadn't found another English teacher doing the Flipped Classroom the way I wanted to do it. I hardly met any English teachers doing it at all. I met April Gudenrath, a high school English teacher from Colorado Springs, at the conference and, although I had a different concept of how I wanted to flip my class, I got some ideas from her. We have since collaborated on several projects related to Flipped Learning. When I made that decision to begin flipping my

English class starting that next school year, there was no way I could fathom the transformative experience to my teaching that was about to happen.

I have learned a lot of lessons about Flipped Learning during the past few years, some by trial and error and some by connecting with any Flipped Learning teacher I could find. Below is a list of some valuable insights I came across. This list is by no means exhaustive, nor in order of importance, but represents the main reasons I continue to flip.

## Flipping Benefits Students of All Abilities

With the Flipped Classroom, I can give struggling students ample attention and assessment to meet their needs. I have the flexibility to give alternate assessments on an individualized level. I have the extra time needed to talk with these students and help them where they are struggling. If they are behind grade level, I can easily modify assignments or teach/reteach missing content. These students also don't feel the embarrassment of being asked to answer questions in front of the class when they don't know the answer, or the embarrassment of having to ask a question in front of the class, when, in their mind, everyone else gets it.

And I wasn't the only one seeing these results. Because of the success Clintondale High School in Michigan was experiencing from flipping its math program, in 2010, it made the decision to flip all its ninth grade classes, including language arts. By the end of that first semester, it saw a 33% drop in failure rates in ELA classes. Even more impressive, by the end of the second year of flipping, students scored 28% higher in writing and 34% higher in reading on the Michigan Merit Exam (Green, 2012).

Struggling students aren't the only students to benefit. One of the first reactions I noticed was the apprehensiveness of my higher-ability students when learning about the Flipped Classroom. These students had success in the old, traditional model and worried they wouldn't continue that success. For many of them, success meant they got As and Bs. However, they quickly saw that not only could I challenge them to go further as students, I could offer them the support they needed to take risks, to go deeper, or to explore a problem further than they ever had. Previously, these students rarely got academic attention from their teachers. Their work was completed well and, even if it exceeded expectations, was marked or given feedback based on the expectation of all students. Now, I could challenge these students to go beyond the grade-level standard. Prior to flipping, I often had students who were very creative and talented writers or readers to whom I couldn't give the time to individualize their feedback. With flipping, I can. I can now have individual discussions with these students and challenge or affirm their observations about a book we're reading. I can challenge them to evaluate their own writing on a higher level. Seventh grader Tanner observed, "When I first heard about the flipped class,

I was very skeptical. I had never had a Flipped Classroom before, and I was worried that it was going to be a lot harder than a normal classroom." However, his final evaluation said, "I currently enjoy having the flipped classroom. It gives me a lot more freedom about what I work on during the week. I like it because we can easily get help from Mr. Cockrum while we are working on it in class instead of emailing him or waiting until the next day to ask him."

## Flipping Helps Students Become More Responsible for Their Own Learning

Flipping your classroom allows you the opportunity to make your classroom more student centered. With the ability to pace themselves, my students became more responsible for their own learning. They not only developed skills in time management by organizing their own daily and weekly schedule, they also were encouraged and supported in finding ways to personalize their learning. Traditional schooling has made students believe they must conform to certain requirements to show learning. When I am able to assess all students individually, they realize that *learning* is the most important goal, not just being able to fill in the blank correctly. When students realize that the learning is what is being evaluated and not whether they completed a checklist of items, they feel empowered to take control of their own learning.

## Flipping Benefits Busy Students

In my classroom, flipping has allowed me to offer multiple assignments in advance. It also allows my students the ability to complete most, if not all, of their work in class. Busy students love being able to control the amount of homework they have. I have a student, Myra, who is a high-level gymnast, and her evenings and weekends are pretty full. She checks with me at the beginning and end of every week to confirm all current and upcoming assignments. She is then able to use her class time efficiently to complete her work in class. She said in her end-of-year survey, "My favorite part of using the Flipped Classroom in English was that I was able to completely manage my work. I could watch videos ahead of classes, and then get ahead if I had lots of activities on a certain day. It helped ease up my schedule and I felt like I was pretty on top of things." Even the students who aren't busy appreciate being able to minimize or even eliminate homework.

## Flipping Allows Teachers More Individual Interaction with Every Student

The biggest benefit of flipping, and the reason I am able to easily individualize or differentiate my instruction, is that I have significantly more interaction time with every student. As Bergmann and Sams often note, in a Flipped Classroom, the teacher can "reach every student in every class every day." In a recent Speak Up survey, nearly 60% of students in grades 6–12 agreed with the statement that Flipped Learning "would be a good way for me to learn" (Project Tomorrow, 2013). I make a priority of having a conversation with each student even if it is not about anything academic. And that individual interaction leads to the next point. Flipped Classrooms are really about relationships.

## Flipping Allows Teachers the Ability to Develop Better Relationships with All Their Students

One of my favorite benefits of the Flipped Classroom is that the amount of individual interaction I get with each student almost instantly creates better relationships with each student. All students want attention, whether they admit it or not. The Flipped Classroom allows me to give all my students individual positive attention. I don't think many people can argue that putting in valuable time talking with each student will not pay major dividends on learning.

Many flipped teachers and students report the same benefit. In a survey of educators and students across the United States, close to 80% of students and 90% of teachers said that positive interactions between teachers and students have increased because of flipping their class (Driscoll, 2012). If this was the only benefit that came from Flipped Learning, it would still be more than worth the time invested. I get to have amazing conversations with my students. I find out their likes and dislikes. I get to know them as people, and not just students that sit in my classroom. This is what I got into teaching to do.

## Flipping Significantly Reduces Negative Behaviors that Affect Classroom Management

As I mentioned earlier, prior to flipping, I felt I was spending a great deal of time tackling classroom management and classroom behavior issues. Admittedly, I wasn't good at behavior management in the classroom. I went to several conferences and tried different methods, but still felt I was falling short. Now, I don't have nearly the behavior issues in my classroom. The students who interrupted class because they were craving attention no longer have an audience. Students who were bored now have challenging activities to fill the class time. Students who felt inadequate because they didn't understand the material now get the help they need. Clintondale High School saw a 74% decrease in student discipline cases during the first two years of flipping all its classes (Green, 2012).

I'll be honest—not all behavior issues magically disappear. However, when a problem arises, I can now deal with that problem individually rather than having to figure out how to manage the classroom while at the same time addressing the unwelcome behavior. And many times, an individual discussion easily solves the problem.

## Flipping Is Not About the Video

Finally, many Flipped Classroom proponents will tell you, "It is not about the video." Well, what does that mean exactly? The majority of new flippers focus much of their attention on creating videos. The content creation process quite possibly generates the highest amount of stress for many teachers. If you've just made the decision to flip or are still considering flipping, you may have some anxiety about creating videos. I get that. Later in this book, I'll give you details on creating videos and some tools to do that. However, I found that the video does not do the teaching. The video provides lower-level content for students in an asynchronous environment. The Flipped Classroom is really about being student centered and flexible with the options you have once you've freed up this class time (Moran & Young, in press). As I've progressed in how I operate my Flipped Classroom, I have made fewer videos. I spend more time developing and creating in-class opportunities for learning. That time is made available, though, because I made the videos initially. If you are wondering what to do with that class time, I provide you several lesson ideas in the coming chapters.

I tell you all this because I was on a quest similar to that of many teachers. I was looking for a better way to teach, a better way for my students to become self-guided learners, and more job satisfaction. I found it all in the Flipped Classroom. And other teachers are as well. In a recent survey of Flipped Classroom teachers, nearly 90% of teachers reported an improvement in their own job satisfaction after flipping their classes (ClassroomWindow and Flipped Learning Network, 2012).

Making the switch isn't easy. It takes the willingness to reevaluate every lesson, every project, every assignment you do. It is a shift for the students too, and it takes them some time to adapt. Just like two dancing partners; if one changes the step, his or her partner will stumble until he or she finds the right step. You'll be changing the dance steps on your students. They will stumble at first, some for longer than others. But they will adapt and be better for it.

As I mentioned earlier, when I started flipping my class, very few English teachers were flipping. Few had even heard of it. Many of my colleagues and collaborators were science and math teachers. As many of you will find, when you flip, your class experiences an upheaval of constant transformation. My class is still evolving. Where I was two years ago is night and day from where I am now. And that is what is so appealing to me and to many other flippers. The constant evaluation and modification makes teaching exciting for me again. The satisfaction of seeing that "Aha!" moment with my students in class, the deeper relationships I can form with every student, and the higher engagement in class from my students all make the process worthwhile.

This book is not only about my journey into Flipped Learning, but also about all I've learned during the past few years adapting the Flipped Classroom to language arts in the hope that you can feel the rewarding experiences that I've had.

Dave Burgess, in his book *Teach Like a Pirate,* uses an excellent peloton reference. In bicycle racing, a peloton is a group or pack of racers that saves energy by riding close together. The method can use as much as 40% less energy for a rider. However, at some point, a rider wants to break away from the peloton and push out into the lead. The peloton then tries to pull the rider back in because that is in its best interest. The same can be said for teaching. Some teachers stay in the peloton because it requires less energy. When one teacher breaks out on his or her own, other teachers consciously or subconsciously try to bring that teacher back into the pack. Don't be afraid to break from the peloton.

## Flipping Your Thoughts: Reflections on What You've Just Read

Before you flip, it is imperative to analyze why you are flipping.

What about flipping is most interesting to you?

Is the extra work worth the potential benefits to your class?

What roadblocks might you encounter in your journey to flip?

Where can you see the addition of technology improving your classroom?

Where can you find inspiration to take the next step?

# 2

# What Is a Flipped Classroom?

This is a common question and the answer is hard to pin down. One of the reasons it is difficult to give a firm definition is that in their book *Flip Your Classroom,* Jon Bergmann and Aaron Sams (2012) write:

> We encourage you to explore and hybridize what you have learned from us, adapting it to what you already know to be good teaching practice. (109)

Because of this adaption and personalization, few Flipped Classrooms look the same. Teachers flip for different reasons. The mass media appears to define flipping the classroom as lecture at home and homework at school, which grossly oversimplifies it. The definition I operate from is this:

> using technology to deliver asynchronous direct instruction with the intention of freeing up class time for student-centered learning.

The ultimate goal of Flipped Learning is to provide a student-centered learning environment. This gives teachers the ability to practice project-based learning, mastery, inquiry, peer instruction, constructivism, and more. The flip makes these pieces possible, but they are not necessarily required to flip.

Some teachers say, "I don't lecture, so I don't need to flip my class." Other opponents of flipping assert that lecture is just bad teaching on video. I prefer to use the term *direct instruction* as opposed to *lecture.* Using the term *lecture,* I believe, conjures up a negative image of that boring math teacher we all had in high school who rambles on with little interaction with the class. That is not what I mean. *Direct instruction* is explicitly teaching a concept or skill. It can be interactive; it can be discussion based. But, if you've found it necessary to stand up in front of the classroom for even a short amount of time, you've found that there is some use for direct instruction. I rarely "lectured" prior to flipping, but did do a lot of direct instruction mini-lessons. Many ELA teachers find they are already closer to flipping than they realized. You may find the same thing. Flipping is just shifting that direct instruction to another setting.

On my podcast, Jon Bergmann defined Flipped Learning as "moving the direct instruction from the public space to the private space" (Bergmann, 2012). A large amount of information and misinformation exists out there. The concept also has different names: *Flipped Classroom, Flipped Teaching, Flipped Learning.* Therefore, I didn't think I could go forward in this book until there was a good understanding of the history of the term and of what a Flipped Classroom really is.

Many people incorrectly believe that Salman Khan coined the term when he used the phrase "flip your class" in his TED talk in 2010 (Khan, 2011). While he may have catapulted the term into exposure, he wasn't the first to use it. As a matter of fact, Jon Bergmann and Aaron Sams, who wrote the book on the Flipped Classroom, didn't create the term either.

The earliest academic research I can find using the term *Flipped* or *Flipping* comes from Wesley Baker (2000). However, his research focused more on learning management systems (LMS) as opposed to technology or video in general. The term didn't make another appearance until Mike Tenneson and Bob McGlasson (2005) and Jeremy Strayer (2007) began presenting research on the term *Flipping* as it is more widely known today.

Around the same time, Bergmann and Sams began creating videos for their chemistry students in Woodland Park, Colorado. In their rural school environment, they had frequent student absences because of their location, and the two were looking for a way to reach their students outside the classroom. Creating videos was the answer. They initially called this idea *Vodcasting.*

During the next few years, they began getting requests to speak to small audiences about their innovative work. It wasn't until 2010 that the term *Flipped Classroom* became associated with Bergmann and Sams. Daniel Pink wrote an article for *The Telegraph* about one of Bergmann and Sams's colleagues, Karl Fisch, and was the first to call the process "Flip-Thinking" (Pink, 2010). As this idea of the Flipped Classroom grew simultaneously with Bergmann and Sams's approach, the two eventually merged into one. In 2012, Bergmann and Sams founded the Flipped Learning Network, a nonprofit organization whose purpose is to guide the discussion on Flipped Learning.

That is the history of Flipped Learning in general. The specific history of Flipped Learning in language arts is more limited. As I mentioned before, prior to me flipping, April Gudenrath was the only identified flipped ELA teacher I could find. I'm not saying such teachers weren't out there; I just couldn't find them using Internet searches, social media, or word of mouth. Which is exactly why I wrote this book; to guide other ELA flippers.

Many iterations of Flipped Learning have emerged. Often requoted, Brian Bennett said, "Flipped Class is an ideology, not a methodology" (Bennett, 2011). The terms for Flipped Learning are still in their infancy. What the concept will grow up to be remains to be seen. Recently, Flipped Classroom proponents have begun to postulate that Flipped Learning is not the "flip" of homework with lecture (although that is where the name originated). It is now more accurately the "flip" of Bloom's Taxonomy. Time shifting some instruction allows students to spend more time in the higher-level process of Bloom's in the presence of their teacher and thus more time in the lower levels of Bloom's outside the classroom. My Flipped Classroom looks much more like that. In Chapter 4, I discuss the different models of flipping that have sprung with this same idea.

I have found components common to all Flipped Classrooms. This is true for any content area. More ELA-specific information is provided in the following chapters. Three main components are required for a classroom to be considered a Flipped Classroom.

## Instruction Delivered Asynchronously

To free up class time for work, teachers need to find a way to deliver instruction asynchronously. Using videos, podcasts, interactive books, and so forth, teachers create content that students can consume at a time of their choosing. This is vital to how a Flipped Classroom works.

## Students Have Immediate and Consistent Access to Information

Students must be able to access the material quickly and efficiently for a Flipped Classroom to succeed. Teachers need to be free to work with all students. The content must be accessible so the students can view it when they need. If the students cannot do that, granting access will take up the teachers' time. Now, I'm not saying teachers shouldn't help students struggling to get access. But students should be given tools to do this on their own.

I should mention that one question frequently asked by those considering the flip is how to get access to all students, even those with limited Internet access at home. That is a valid concern, but it is definitely possible to resolve it. In Chapter 11, I cover the options in one of the FAQs.

## Teachers Are Available during Class Time to Answer Questions and to Guide Learning

Finally, providing the instruction outside of class time allows teachers to be available for students during class time. Ideally, teachers will have students doing activities that require higher-level thinking skills. If teachers are using videos with the intention of getting more time to lecture, then it is not a Flipped Classroom. The class time gained from eliminating direct instruction still needs to be valuable time. You won't be sitting down during this time. You will be actively helping, working with, and guiding students constantly. Flipped teachers are not "film-strip teachers." Planning what happens during that class time becomes not only the most integral, but also the most rewarding part of a successful Flipped Classroom experience.

The Flipped Classroom is a grassroots movement of teachers searching for a better way to teach. Therefore, what Flipped Learning means (to me) is something that works for my teaching style in my classroom for my students. It is not what defines me or my class. It is not the only method/technique/tool that I use. But, most important, Flipped Learning causes me to reevaluate every lesson I do to see if there is a better way.

## Flipping Your Thoughts: Reflections on What You've Just Read

While many of the ideas of Flipped Learning aren't new, the terminology is.

Has your definition of a Flipped Classroom changed? If so, how?

Did this chapter clear up misconceptions you had about flipping?

What information can you use from this chapter to explain flipping to others?

The Flipped Classroom is very much a grassroots movement by teachers.

Do you find value in this being a grassroots movement?

If you are already flipping, what can you do to help the movement progress?

# 3

# Why a Flipped Class Works in Language Arts

This may be the chapter many of you have been waiting to read. I'm going to reveal the "secrets" to why Flipped Learning works in a language arts classroom. The reasons it works in an ELA class are the same reasons it works in other content areas. Teachers often compartmentalize classes and do not realize we are teaching a lot of the same skills across the different subject and content areas. Those skills are the high-order skills—those twenty-first-century skills of critical thinking and problem solving, communication, collaboration, and creativity and innovation. These are the skills that flipping allows each teacher to spend time developing. That said, I think flipping an ELA class brings many benefits that may or may not be seen in other subject areas.

I'm not saying every teacher needs to flip his or her class. There are some amazing teachers in the teaching profession who can accomplish all they need to accomplish in their classrooms in a wonderfully engaging way and who don't need to flip. I could not accomplish all I needed to accomplish in the short time I had my students with me in class. I could not consistently hold their attention and keep them engaged for an entire period. Whether because of my delivery style or the content I was presenting, I wasn't hooking the students. I needed the flip. I was not a dynamic speaker. I was not good at managing behavior. With the flip, I didn't need to be. Sure, your videos should be somewhat engaging and have a reflection piece, but they only need to be delivered once. Delivering a lesson over the course of five or six class periods a day can be extremely tiring and I'm sure that shows to the students. Flipping allowed me to be more engaged and focused with my students, which benefited both my students and me. I'm not saying simply flipping your class will make a bad teacher good. But the internal reflection process needed, the constant self-evaluation, the flexibility in teaching flipping requires are steps to improving any teacher, good or bad.

There also isn't a need to flip every lesson. Some teachers flip a lesson or unit. However, I believe that once you begin the process of flipping, it is difficult to stop. It just becomes part of what you do. I don't even think of my lessons and units in terms of how I will flip them anymore. I just see where it fits. If it doesn't fit, I don't flip.

I refer to my classroom now as sloppy. I believe strongly in what Dave Burgess calls *creative alchemy* (Burgess, 2012). Put a lot of common, unrelated things together and come up with something great. My class is the writing process in action. Each lesson, I have an idea of where I want to go, but as students construct their knowledge in the classroom, as I construct my knowledge in the classroom, I weave, change pace, jump back, accelerate forward, slow down, or do what is needed to meet the needs of my students. The lesson plans I present later in this book are ideal situations. In reality, I may have to modify each lesson for each class a few times in a single class period based on need. I customize the lesson for the students. However, I know other English teachers who are very organized and structured. That is their style of teaching. Or maybe their administration requires more structure in the classroom. If that is the case, flipping still works. Bergmann and Sams like to say in their book, "Flipping your class isn't for control freaks" (Bergmann & Sams, 2012). I don't think that is necessarily true. Yes, you do give some amount of control over to your students. It truly is a student-centered model when done effectively. I probably give a lot more than other teachers do. But, when you flip your class, structure it to fit your teaching style.

That being said, there are several reasons the flip works in many English classrooms.

## Individualized Instruction

The research shows that writing instruction is best when it is personalized and content oriented (Graham & Perin, 2007). It is amazingly rewarding when I can sit down with all my students and discuss their writing one on one. They can ask questions. I can ask them specific questions. I can invest the time in each student because I now have the time. I do still read some papers and give feedback outside of class time. Because my students are conditioned to watch videos and use technology, many times I'll give audio feedback as well (more on that later). But the amount I read outside of class has been significantly reduced. And, therefore, I'm able to focus more of my attention on the quality of the feedback I give. Seventh grader Rachel said, "I can now understand lessons better and I can watch the videos multiple times if I need to. During the class, I can ask questions instead of trying to make time before or after school." Another seventh grader, Moira, said, "I think it made learning easier, because I learned at my own pace, and because I kept my focus much better with the videos, rather than a classroom lesson."

## Community

I constantly tell my students, "We are a community of writers." One often over-looked benefit of a Flipped Classroom is that students have time to collaborate with each other. My students are constantly reading and revising each other's work, brainstorming ideas together, and making the writing process communal. One student even had the idea of making a sign that said, "I am available to peer edit" that she placed on her desk. I have a "three-then-me" policy for my students. They are encouraged to have three other students critique their work before they show it to me. They can receive input from students or adults outside the class, but are encouraged to use their classmates. With Google Docs Revision History, I can easily check who collaborated on a document. The important thing is the students become a community. They want to work together and help each other. They are all invested in each other's success. They also see me as part of that community and not just an all-knowing disseminator of content. And they now have more class time to work together and keep the community vibrant.

Seventh grader Myra observed, "I like how we peer edit A LOT. I feel like it gives me more time to check over it and get more feedback before I turn in the final draft." Seventh grader Delia added, "I really like the peer editing process. It helps me know what to look for specifically in writing, whether it's my own or someone else's. It also shows me how to cater to the age group I'm targeting; I trust my peers' opinions and generally think that their suggestions are helpful."

## Self-Pacing

Genius doesn't spark everyone at the same time. I want my students to embrace the creative process. I do have deadlines that must be met, so I call my class *guided pacing*, as opposed to totally self-paced. However, when students work on what is up to them. If their creativity isn't sparked that day during that class period, they work on something that may require lower-level skills, like watching a video or completing grammar exercises. They may check a nearly completed assignment for grammar and mechanics. Some will choose to work on an independent project because that can ignite interest in them. Others will storm into my room beaming with energy. They are enthusiastic to get working right away because they just can't wait to get their ideas out on paper. Imagine if I asked them to bottle that enthusiasm and work on the specific assignment I had planned for that day. Imagine the quality of work I would get from the unenthused students if I asked them to write something that required a lot of passionate ideas. None of these students would perform their best. Flipping allows my students the freedom to choose what they want to work on when. And, when I see a student with unbridled enthusiasm, I can release the reins and let them run with it. When I see a student with motivation problems, I can discuss and problem solve with that student. The students aren't bound to wait for me to give any direct instruction and I am not tied to that either.

One of my seventh graders, Tanner, said in his end-of-the-year survey, "My favorite part of the flipped class is all the freedom and the choices I can make about what I can work on." Another seventh grader, Kate, added, "I like it because it gives us freedom to decide what we want to work on that day and we have to plan our time to get it all done."

## Choice in Activities/Alternate Assessment

The ability to individualize instruction also gives me the ability to individualize assessments. I can offer my students multiple options in how they show learning. I believe everything is writing. A presentation, a note to a friend, an essay, a story, an advertisement, a song, acting, improvisation—they all require a process. I teach a "writing" process that can be applied to nearly everything we do. Therefore, when I teach concepts, students aren't constrained to one way of showing me understanding. Don't want to write a persuasive essay to show me persuasion? Mock up some advertising, create a public service announcement (PSA), write a newspaper editorial, just show me you understand persuasion. I give students some parameters they need to meet in order to "prove" understanding, usually in rubric form. The requirements are objective based and not assignment based, so I'm assessing the skill and not arbitrary things like transitions between slides. The students' goal then is to show proof of understanding the objective. They can't simply write the definition on a note card and expect that to pass. They need to show a link between skill and application. The choice needs to be intentional. Many will choose the assignment I've set up for them because that is what years of schooling has taught them. But not all will. Students always surprise me with their creativity. This allows the student who likes anime to keep drawing (while at the same time writing) and the student who likes math to build a Web site from the programming side (while at the same time writing). Choice in assessment is made possible by flipping.

## Focus on the "Fun Stuff"

We've all probably said it (or wanted to say it) at least once in our career: "Students, I know this is boring, but we have to get through it." Let's hope we've only said it once. Put this material on video. Now, I'm not saying your videos have to be dull and boring. I give you some tips later on about making engaging videos. For me, the "fun stuff" is the activities we do, the application of the material, and watching the students grow and make deep connections to the material. With a Flipped Classroom, that is what I get to do every day—the "fun stuff."

For example, I used to hate teaching grammar. While I come by it naturally, many students do not. Explaining grammar rules over and over again seemed to wear on me. Now, it is entirely different. The videos cover the grammar rules. If a student forgets or needs it re-explained, he or she can re-watch the video. I get to plan activities and discussions that help the grammar stick. Now, instead of me giving direct instruction on grammar, my students are having a lively discussion on whys and hows of grammar in different situations; they are helping each other understand, building that knowledge base as a group. I was stunned this past school year when one of my English classes requested we have a class day each week devoted to grammar, like it was some sort of reward. That would have never happened prior to me flipping my class.

## Grading

I remember a conversation I had with a former math teacher about grading. During the discussion, I showed him a rubric that I use and explained how I assess each point in the rubric. After I finished, he asked how long it took me. I told him on average maybe 20 minutes per paper. His next question was, "And you do this for every paper?" We as English teachers know the amount of time we spend grading papers. Post flip, I take significantly fewer papers home to grade at the end of the day. Often it is none. I don't want to say that I don't still work hard. I just work harder in different areas. When I assess students' work, I'm often able to read it in class with them. I can give them feedback immediately. If I want more time to digest it, I'll make myself a note to read it during my plan period or after school.

Another benefit is that my feedback is more targeted and richer. I'm not reading stacks of papers in one or two sittings trying to give students feedback. And, with the rise in collaborative technologies, I can give audio feedback, keep a record of written feedback, and more.

## Efficiently Use Time

Some skills can be taught in a relatively short time frame. However, many ELA skills cannot be. While we can teach the basics of MLA formatting, for instance, in a few classes, teaching proper research skills takes much longer. With the flip, I can shorten the time needed to teach many of these skills. I'm sitting there with the students as they're doing their research. I'm helping them ask the right questions as they synthesize sources. This contact with each student allows the entire class to move through the content more efficiently with deeper understanding. I can't say there is a hard and fast rule, but I would estimate each unit takes 25% less time to complete. But saving that time is not worthwhile if the students aren't learning the material. I can confidently say that they are more engaged in the process and learn it much better at a level I didn't see before flipping, even with the shortened time frame.

Reading text takes less time as well. Teachers can structure their reading units in a way that makes more efficient use of class time and thus lessens the time needed to read a text. Plays can be performed in class more easily and any direct instruction needed can be offloaded to video. Reading can be done in class wrapped around activities designed to enhance understanding, and it makes the process more enjoyable for students and teachers. My first full year of flipping, I actually got into the fourth quarter and had run out of content I was required to cover. I was able to get creative with project ideas and activities that I never had time for in the past. I now pace my curriculum accordingly, allowing time for extension activities, autonomous projects, passion-based learning, and more.

## Autonomous Learning

A Flipped Classroom is student-centered and can create very autonomous learners. With the model, teaching students how to learn becomes a big part of the instruction. Teachers can now spend the time to talk with their students about choices they make in their own learning process. Students have a larger responsibility to manage their own time and, with necessary support, can learn crucial time management strategies.

Seventh grader Moira said, "I think my responsibility has really improved because I really am pushed to be responsible with watching the videos, writing the papers, and doing the class work." She also added, "I found the class a bit more stressful because we had a ton more responsibility, but it was more fun and we got more freedom." I find it interesting that a student can find a class "more stressful" and "more fun" at the same time!

## Common Core State Standards

Many states are going to the Common Core State Standards (CCSS) with a goal of having students college and career ready. The Flipped Classroom gives teachers the ability to address many of the skills required in CCSS. In addition, the Council of Writing Program Administrators produced a document describing the attributes, what it calls "Habits of Mind," writers need to be college and career ready. The work outlines the following skills: Curiosity, Openness, Engagement, Creativity, Persistence, Responsibility, Flexibility, and Metacognition (Council of Writing Program Administrators, 2011). These skills fit hand in hand with the spirit of a Flipped Classroom.

- Curiosity: Students have the freedom and are encouraged to explore their curiosities in what they learn, the writing they produce, and the topics they research.
- Openness: Students have the opportunity to be open to multiple ideas and ways of thinking.
- Engagement: Students are more engaged in the class material, their work, and the outcome of their learning.
- Creativity: Students have the freedom and are encouraged to look at problems, projects, and research from a different perspective and come up with a variety of approaches.
- Persistence: Students gain skills in managing and finishing long- and short-term projects.
- Responsibility: Especially in a guided or self-paced classroom, but in all Flipped Classrooms, students gain valuable self-reliance skills and responsibility. As Moira said, she had "a ton more responsibility."
- Flexibility: This is a keystone of a Flipped Classroom. Flexibility by the teacher is crucial for success in flipping. However, in the process, students learn that flexibility is important as well. Students become very good at adapting to many situations, projects, and problems.
- Metacognition: Many teachers go to the Flipped Classroom to help students think more about their learning. In a Flipped Classroom, teachers can guide students to think about their learning and how they construct knowledge.

I honestly can't imagine going back to teaching an ELA classroom without flipping. It is that transformative of an experience. I get to have fun with my students. I get to plan exciting and engaging lessons. I get to have conversations with all my students about real, authentic applications of ideas. The freedom and rewards I now feel as a teacher are because of the environment flipping has helped me create. It takes time. It took me months to build a class that worked for my students and me. It constantly evolves and gets better all the time. I can't express emphatically enough how much this change has revolutionized my teaching. Seventh grader Rachel sums it up best, "Flipped classroom just makes everything easier."

**Flipping Your Thoughts: Reflections on What You've Just Read**

Many people say you can't flip a language arts class. What do you think?

Do you feel more confident now about the possibilities of flipping an ELA classroom?

Do you find value in creating a community of writers?

Have you been looking for ways to give students more valuable feedback on their work?

Have you been able to create the same environment without flipping?

# 4

# Models of a Flipped Classroom

One of the biggest surprises to a lot of teachers new to the Flipped Classroom is the variety of models of flipping. You see, flipping isn't a model in itself, but a guiding principle of how you wish to deliver content and direct instruction. Everyone's flip looks different based on teaching style, students, and other factors. As more and more teachers begin to flip their classes, consistent models are emerging. I have identified five different models in use in English classes across the country. I've divided them into First and Second Iteration Flips. The majority of teachers start in the First Iteration Flips and progress in their practice to the Second Iteration Flips. I use a mixture of all the models, as do others, depending on what works best for the unit I am teaching. Don't feel the need to constrain yourself to one of the models discussed here. Pick and choose what works best for the lesson/day/unit you are working on. The best part about flipped strategies is that they are flexible.

## First Iteration Flips

### TRADITIONAL FLIP

This is the first and most prominent flip. The Traditional Flip is simply front-loading a video of content followed by problems, activities, or writing in class based on that content. For the most part, when the media refer to the Flipped Classroom, this is what they mean. This is where nearly every flipper starts his or her journey. It is simplest to understand because it breaks flipping down into a linear process.

This is also the most criticized model, especially in the humanities. Few English teachers give large segments of class time to direct instruction. Therefore, they don't see this model as more effective than what they are already doing. I agree. This isn't a dynamic, engaging, groundbreaking model that is going to revolutionize education or even writing instruction. However, for the teacher who has struggled with innovation in the classroom, for the teacher who has resisted or feared new technologies, or for the teacher who is looking for a way to maximize class time and doesn't know where to start, this is the model for them. Some teachers stay in this model six months, some can stay for a year or more, but eventually all move on.

Truth be told, even though I don't believe this is the most effective method of flipping an English classroom, I recommend most teachers start here. Even if it is for just a few units, it is a good way to get down a video delivery process while at the same time exploring what Flipped Learning can provide for your class.

## WRITING WORKSHOP FLIP

Another common way English teachers flip is to modify the Writing Workshop model made popular by Lucy Calkins (1986). The Writing Workshop endorses many philosophies shared by flipped teachers, including that students should be writing in class, working in class, making choices personal to them, and having the teacher model and guide. Many English teachers find the Writing Workshop to be very effective in writing instruction. There is also a variation called the Reading Writing Workshop (Atwell, 1998) that incorporates reading skills. I had a Writing Workshop in my classroom for two years prior to flipping. I retain many Writing Workshop elements in my Flipped Classroom.

The structure of a Writing Workshop is as follows (Calkins, 1986):

1. A consistent signal at the beginning of the Writing Workshop.
2. A direct instruction mini-lesson. The mini-lesson should connect to previous lessons, teach or demonstrate a new writing technique, and allow students to practice the technique with the supervision of the teacher.
3. The mini-lesson is followed by writing time in class. During this time, the teacher has writing conferences or meets with small groups and gives more specific instruction.
4. The class concludes with students sharing their work with each other.

When I followed the Writing Workshop model, I had difficulty fitting all that into my allotted class time. The Writing Workshop model ideally uses *a minimum* of 50 minutes of class time. I had 40-minute classes. The Writing Workshop Flip would remove the mini-lesson from this list and replace it with video instruction. That time is then freed up from the classroom and students have more writing and sharing time in the classroom.

This flip is a good starting point for teachers already using the Writing Workshop model or some variation of it. Similar to starting with a Traditional Flip, it allows teachers time to practice with video instruction and to develop a creation and distribution process that will work for their class.

## Second Iteration Flips

The following are known as Second Iteration Flips. This means that teachers traditionally start in one of the first two flips and evolve into a more complex, more dynamic flip as they reflect and revise their practice. This conversion of practice is what caused Bergmann and Sams to begin using the terminology of Flipped *Learning* as opposed to Flipped *Classroom*.

### EXPLORE-FLIP-APPLY

This is the model I use most frequently in my classroom. This model is derived from the work of Ramsey Musallam and is a variation on the Explore-Explain-Apply model (Musallam, 2011). Musallam describes the most important element of this model as "the intentional withholding of knowledge" (Musallam & Highfill, 2013). The reasoning behind this method is that when in the learning cycle the teacher delivers the video is important to the instruction's effectiveness. Research shows placing the video later in the learning cycle (as opposed to the beginning) after some activities enhances learning (Schneider et al., 2013).

The model is a series of steps designed to reveal knowledge as the students construct or discover it. Withholding that information from the start until the students are perplexed enough to really desire that information is the key component of locking in the information and truly learning it. If the model had a linear progression, it would look like this:

1. **Explore Stage:** Students are presented with an activity, problem, event, or task in which they engage in an exploratory process to discover the knowledge required. It might be a brainstorming activity or a writing problem. The teacher observes and intentionally does not intervene, allowing students to construct and explore their own knowledge. The Explore stage should ideally go on until the students can no longer progress without certain information and have sufficiently stressed their cognitive load. I have some Explore stages that last just 10–15 minutes and others that go on for a couple of days. If students have the knowledge or are gaining the knowledge on their own, there is no need for the teacher to intervene.

2. **Flip Stage:** Once the students have reached the extent of the Explore stage and need the teacher to inject information, the video instruction is utilized. A short video based on observations during the Explore stage delivers necessary content on an as-needed basis. At this point, the teacher adds content, confirms discoveries, clears up misconceptions, and guides the students into the next stage. I may confirm some vocabulary or elaborate on a skill the students were close to getting. Providing the video at this point in the process

allows the teacher to make the content in the video much more focused and class specific.

3. **Apply Stage:** Once the content has been delivered in the Flip stage, students can move into an exercise or assignment in which they apply, in a different manner, the material they learned from the previous two stages. Some units may have a series of Explore-Flips before they make it to the Apply stage. A teacher may also insert practice in between Flip and Apply so that students can practice a skill more before they are assessed on it.

## FLIP-MASTERY

This model was Bergmann and Sams's second iteration of their flip. The Flip-Mastery model combines flipped videos with mastery instruction. In this model, students watch the videos and complete assignments at their own pace. In addition, students cannot move on to the next unit until they have reached the teacher-defined mastery of specific skills. Teachers may base those skills on Common Core State Standards and define mastery that way, or they may have their own standardized definition of mastery. In any regard, the determination of what qualifies as mastery is the guide for assessment.

The lure of a self-paced environment can be very attractive. I do what I call *guided pacing*. I allow my students to choose and work on their assignments at their own pace. However, I have set deadlines for work and allow students to move on to the next unit even if they didn't achieve mastery. The benefits of mastery can be debated, but I will not do that here. The autonomy created by video instruction in the Flipped Classroom makes mastery possible.

In a math or science class, mastery may be more easily identified. Teachers can give a test with explicitly correct answers. In English, it may not seem as straightforward. Some teachers use a standards-based rubric model to determine mastery. Others use objectives-based grading to define mastery for their students.

This model requires the teacher to be a well-versed content expert. Even without mastery, the self-pacing or guided pacing puts many students at different points in the learning process. In my class, at any given time, students could complete five or six different activities or assignments most days. In that scenario, a teacher needs to be able to discuss any multitude of topics that come up during class time. This also requires a teacher to be organized. Keeping track of where each student is in the learning journey is vital to assure they are making appropriate progress. Some teachers use technology like a Google Form, spreadsheet, or a blog. Others may use a clipboard or notepad and hand write everything. I've found the clipboard method works best for me, but have also used an iPad to track work and minimize paper use. I do have a daily blog to remind the students what they need to be working on. It's really up to you what style works best. However, if you choose this model, be prepared to initially feel very overwhelmed. Have a solid organization method in place from the start and tweak it as necessary after you've seen it in practice. I would say the main thing for implementing this model successfully is having a clearly definable goal of what mastery looks like and communicating that with your students and their parents. If you define mastery as "I'll know it when I see it," students will become quickly discouraged and confused and you won't have their buy-in.

## PEER INSTRUCTION (PI) FLIP

This model is the brainchild of Dr. Eric Mazur at Harvard. Mazur began developing this model in the early 1990s under the premise that students do a pre-class reading or other preparations before coming to class in order to make his class time more effective (Mazur, 1997). Mazur also began to experiment with multimedia content similar to video instruction as early as 1988 (Schell, 2013). More recently, many teachers have been using elements of PI and adding flipping to the mix. If you are not familiar with PI, here are the seven basic steps of the model (Mazur, 1997):

1.  Students get a pre-class activity, often a reading, but in the case of flipping it could be a video or podcast.
2.  At the start of class, the teacher asks the class a question based on the pre-class activity. The question should be at a higher level of processing and should not have a simple, easy-to-identify answer. The question could even be ambiguous enough to not have a right or wrong answer.
3.  Students use their base knowledge to decide on their answer.
4.  The teacher reviews the students' answers through a response system, show of hands, or other quickly accessible method.
5.  Students are then asked to find someone who answered differently from them and discuss why they chose the answer they chose. In this stage, students try to convince the other student they have the correct answer and why. This is the step where students really explore their knowledge and understanding and determine if they answered correctly or not.
6.  Students are then asked again to commit to an answer.
7.  The teacher then reviews the correct answer, gives an explanation of the concept, and determines if more instruction is needed.

The flip in the flipped peer instruction model can come in the first step as a pre-class video. Depending on the complexity of the concept being taught, the flip could also come as an online discussion or facilitated video comments in step 5.

I use this model quite often with grammar instruction. My students can have a pretty lively discussion about parts of a sentence or parts of speech. Asking a student to not only identify a type of phrase, for instance, but also defend why they believe that makes for some very interesting conversations and really locks in the learning. Watching students argue over a gerund phrase is wonderful!

After participating in a combination of peer instruction and Explore-Flip-Apply for one lesson, seventh grader Delia noted, "I did like the discussion process better than the video delivery [first] because I felt like I understood the video better than I would have, and getting a chance to hear my peers' ideas that were different than mine also helped my [assignment]."

## Third Iteration Flips

Where these models will go next is only conjecture. I am encouraged and excited that many of the newer Flipped Learning models have veered toward inquiry and project-based learning. As more research is completed, we are finding Flipped Learning to be an effective method of teaching. As the previous models are explored and revised, a wave of Third Iteration Flips will begin coming down the pipeline. I am amazed all the time at what innovative teachers are adding to their Flipped Classrooms. I'm not even sure we'll stay at Third Iteration very long. The spirit of a Flipped Classroom is innovation and individualization. With that as your guiding principle, there is no limit to the evolution of Flipped Learning.

Many English teachers are already using parts of these models and Blended Learning. Adding a flip for a lot of English teachers isn't really that far of a stretch. As I said before, I use a mixture of several models depending on what I feel works best for the unit. I know other teachers who focus almost primarily on one model. That's entirely up to you. Again, I recommend you start with a First Iteration Flip, but that is only a recommendation, not a requirement. I say that because not only does the teacher need to adjust to the new style, the students need to adjust as well. But, once you and your class get your dancing shoes on, so to speak, you can move into any of the Second Iteration Flips or possibly even invent your own. Flipping then becomes a very beautiful thing.

### Flipping Your Thoughts: Reflections on What You've Just Read

How do you see flipped models evolving?

Did it surprise you to learn there are different models of flipping?

Do the models of flipping confuse people or make flipping better?

Which model of flip ping best fits your teaching style?

Do you have some innovative ideas for a Third Iteration Flip?

# 5

# Flipped Writing Instruction

## What Does a Flipped English Class Look Like?

I get this question often. I will show you examples of what Flipped Instruction can look like, starting with writing instruction. Writing seems to be the place where a lot of ELA teachers begin their flipping experience. The skills needed for writing can be explained in a video and individual instruction with the students can improve those skills. As discussed previously, different models of Flipped Learning are available, and the model you choose determines what your flip looks like. Everyone's flip operates differently based on his or her teaching style, personality, pedagogical influences, and the students in the class. I'll show you a variety of lesson plans for the different models of flipping. Some teachers will use Traditional Flip, some Explore-Flip-Apply, and some Peer Instruction Flip; some will present a similar lesson in two different models. There are no Flip-Mastery lessons here, because the mastery part is in how you assess and not in how you plan your lessons. If you are interested in the Flip-Mastery model, you would take Traditional Flip lessons and add an assessment to the end to determine the students' mastery level.

# Writing Lesson Plan (Traditional Flip)

## HOW CAN A SOURCE BE RELIABLE?

**Topic:** Research Source Reliability

**Grade Level:** 6–12

**Skills:** Research Writing Skills

**Established Goals:** Common Core State Standards

*CCSS.ELA-Literacy.W.5.7* Conduct short research projects that use several sources to build knowledge through investigation of different aspects of a topic.

*CCSS.ELA-Literacy.W.6.1* Write arguments to support claims with clear reasons and relevant evidence.

*CCSS.ELA-Literacy.W.6.2* Write informative/explanatory texts to examine a topic and convey ideas, concepts, and information through the selection, organization, and analysis of relevant content.

*CCSS.ELA-Literacy.W.7.2* Write informative/explanatory texts to examine a topic and convey ideas, concepts, and information through the selection, organization, and analysis of relevant content.

*CCSS.ELA-Literacy.W.7.7* Conduct short research projects to answer a question, drawing on several sources and generating additional related, focused questions for further research and investigation.

*CCSS.ELA-Literacy.W.8.1* Write arguments to support claims with clear reasons and relevant evidence.

*CCSS.ELA-Literacy.W.8.6* Use technology, including the Internet, to produce and publish writing and present the relationships between information and ideas efficiently as well as to interact and collaborate with others.

*CCSS.ELA-Literacy.W.8.7* Conduct short research projects to answer a question (including a self-generated question), drawing on several sources and generating additional related, focused questions that allow for multiple avenues of exploration.

*CCSS.ELA-Literacy.W.9–10.7* Conduct short as well as more sustained research projects to answer a question (including a self-generated question) or solve a problem; narrow or broaden the inquiry when appropriate; synthesize multiple sources on the subject, demonstrating understanding of the subject under investigation.

*CCSS.ELA-Literacy.W.9–10.6* Use technology, including the Internet, to produce, publish, and update individual or shared writing products, taking advantage of technology's capacity to link to other information and to display information flexibly and dynamically.

*CCSS.ELA-Literacy.W.11–12.7* Conduct short as well as more sustained research projects to answer a question (including a self-generated question) or solve a problem; narrow or broaden the inquiry when appropriate; synthesize multiple sources on the subject, demonstrating understanding of the subject under investigation.

*CCSS.ELA-Literacy.W.11–12.8* Gather relevant information from multiple authoritative print and digital sources, using advanced searches effectively; assess the strengths and limitations of each source in terms of the task, purpose, and audience; integrate information into the text selectively to maintain the flow of ideas, avoiding plagiarism and overreliance on any one source and following a standard format for citation.

## Essential Question

What variables go into determining the reliability of a source used in research?

## Objectives

| *Students will understand . . .* | *Students will know . . .* | *Students will . . .* |
|---|---|---|
| ■ efficient ways to search on the Internet. | ■ the importance of attributing Internet sources, and practice a format for citation of sources. | ■ assess the reliability and validity of a source;<br>■ consider and discuss the nature of the Internet, comparing it with more traditional information sources. |

## Assessment Evidence

### Performance Tasks:

- Students will evaluate the reliability of a source on a topic in which they already have a good amount of background knowledge.

- Students will rewrite a Wikipedia Web site using the edit features and adding more credible information as they see needed.

- Students will share their thinking during school lessons and in a journal or a Google Form.

### Self-Assessments:

- Student journals and in-class discussions.

### Other Evidence:

- Rewritten work checked for understanding and accuracy of content and presentation of the content.

## Learning Plan

*Lesson is based on 40-minute class periods but can be modified to fit your needs.*

## Flip

Video assigned as homework or for students to watch in class

Video Topic: How to determine source reliability and validity

## In Class

### Day 1: After students have watched the video:

- Students will pull up a favorite topic on Wikipedia (wikipedia.org). It should be something they know or have read a lot about previously. Examples include favorite athletes, bands, sports, celebrities, and hobbies.

  Modification note: The entire class could do the same Wikipedia page if having enough devices is an issue. The teacher could display the site using a projector or print several copies to distribute paper versions of a Wikipedia page.

- Students will informally assess the reliability and validity of the source using their own criteria.
- Students will write a reflection paragraph or fill in a Google Form.
- Students will use guided notes or a checklist to again assess the reliability and validity.
- The teacher is available to circulate and answer questions as needed.

## Day 2:

- Students will use Wikipedia's editing capabilities to correct any incorrect information. If they cannot find incorrect information, they should find other, unlisted sources that support information. Using the edit features on the site, students will revise the Wikipedia entry to make it more detailed and accurate and add their own reliable sources to the document. The teacher is available to circulate and answer questions as needed.

Modification note: Students could handwrite their revisions if using or having enough computing devices is not possible. It is important for this activity to take place in class.

## Day 3:

Students will begin the next lesson of the unit by watching a video either in class or as homework, which would consist of finding and evaluating sources for the topic of their own research project.

## Reflection Methods

- Students will journal or do another reflective exercise (Google Form) on the choices they made in determining their sources and revisions.
- Students will share their thinking and lessons learned in class discussions and journals.

## Materials

| **Facilities:** | **Equipment (non-tech):** | **Equipment (tech):** |
| --- | --- | --- |
| ■ classroom or computer lab | ■ printouts of Web sites if devices unavailable | ■ device to view flipped video lesson<br>■ device to access Internet sites |

# Writing Lesson Plan (Explore-Flip-Apply)

## HOW CAN A SOURCE BE RELIABLE?

Note: This lesson is similar to the previous lesson, but an Explore activity has been added at the beginning to determine students' previous knowledge and to give students an opportunity to construct new knowledge independently.

**Topic:** Research Source Reliability

**Grade Level:** 6–12

**Skills:** Research Writing Skills

**Established Goals:** Common Core State Standards

*CCSS.ELA-Literacy.W.5.7* Conduct short research projects that use several sources to build knowledge through investigation of different aspects of a topic.

*CCSS.ELA-Literacy.W.6.1* Write arguments to support claims with clear reasons and relevant evidence.

*CCSS.ELA-Literacy.W.6.2* Write informative/explanatory texts to examine a topic and convey ideas, concepts, and information through the selection, organization, and analysis of relevant content.

*CCSS.ELA-Literacy.W.7.2* Write informative/explanatory texts to examine a topic and convey ideas, concepts, and information through the selection, organization, and analysis of relevant content.

*CCSS.ELA-Literacy.W.7.7* Conduct short research projects to answer a question, drawing on several sources and generating additional related, focused questions for further research and investigation.

*CCSS.ELA-Literacy.W.8.1* Write arguments to support claims with clear reasons and relevant evidence.

*CCSS.ELA-Literacy.W.8.6* Use technology, including the Internet, to produce and publish writing and present the relationships between information and ideas efficiently as well as to interact and collaborate with others.

*CCSS.ELA-Literacy.W.8.7* Conduct short research projects to answer a question (including a self-generated question), drawing on several sources and generating additional related, focused questions that allow for multiple avenues of exploration.

*CCSS.ELA-Literacy.W.9–10.7* Conduct short as well as more sustained research projects to answer a question (including a self-generated question) or solve a problem; narrow or broaden the inquiry when appropriate; synthesize multiple sources on the subject, demonstrating understanding of the subject under investigation.

*CCSS.ELA-Literacy.W.9–10.6* Use technology, including the Internet, to produce, publish, and update individual or shared writing products, taking advantage of technology's capacity to link to other information and to display information flexibly and dynamically.

*CCSS.ELA-Literacy.W.11–12.7* Conduct short as well as more sustained research projects to answer a question (including a self-generated question) or solve a problem; narrow or broaden the inquiry when appropriate; synthesize multiple sources on the subject, demonstrating understanding of the subject under investigation.

*CCSS.ELA-Literacy.W.11–12.8* Gather relevant information from multiple authoritative print and digital sources, using advanced searches effectively; assess the strengths and limitations of each source in terms of the task, purpose, and audience; integrate information into the text selectively to maintain the flow of ideas, avoiding plagiarism and overreliance on any one source and following a standard format for citation.

## Essential Question

What variables go into determining the reliability of a source used in research?

## Objectives

| *Students will understand . . .* | *Students will know . . .* | *Students will . . .* |
|---|---|---|
| ■ efficient ways to search on the Internet. | ■ the importance of attributing Internet sources, and practice a format for citation of sources. | ■ assess the reliability and validity of a source;<br>■ consider and discuss the nature of the Internet, comparing it with more traditional information sources. |

## Assessment Evidence

### Performance Tasks:

- Students will evaluate the reliability of a source on a topic in which they already have a good amount of background knowledge.

- Students will rewrite a Wikipedia Web site using the editing features and adding more credible information as they see needed.

- Students will share their thinking during school lessons and in a journal or a Google Form.

### Self-Assessments:

- Student journals and in-class discussions.

### Other Evidence:

- Rewritten work checked for understanding and accuracy of content and presentation of the content.

## Learning Plan

*Lesson is based on 40-minute class periods but can be modified to fit your needs.*

### Day 1: Explore:

Driving Question: How can we determine the reliability of a source?

- Students pull up the Web site allaboutexplorers.com or another Web site that looks "reliable" and professional but contains incorrect information. The Web site could be pulled up on each individual device, displayed on a projector, or printed and distributed.
- Ask the students to give general impressions of the site either in group discussion or in free write exercise.
- Students then select an explorer and read about that person.

Modification note: The teacher (or a student) could read aloud about one pre-chosen explorer.

- Students then discuss or free write their impressions of the information. Depending on the age and ability level, some students may believe the information on the site and not question it. The teacher would work with the group to generate questions about the information guiding the students toward the Driving Question.

**Flip:** Brief video discussing the Driving Question. Students begin to generate a list of need-to-know questions. They can submit these through a Google Form or write them if that's what your class has available.

### Day 2: Explore

- Students will pull up a favorite topic on Wikipedia It should be something they know or have read a lot about previously. Examples include favorite athletes, bands, sports, celebrities, and hobbies.

Modification note: The entire class could do the same Wikipedia page if having enough devices is an issue. The teacher could display the site using a projector or print several copies to distribute paper versions of a Wikipedia page.

- Place the students in small groups and have them discuss the information on their site.
- As a group, students will begin discussing what they need to know and what they already know to determine the reliability of their Wikipedia page.
- Share as a large group what the smaller groups discussed.

**Flip:** Video reviewing the class-generated need-to-know questions; revise or add to them as necessary. This would also be a time to clear up misconceptions and guide students' understanding.

### Day 3: Apply

- Students will use Wikipedia's editing capabilities to correct any incorrect information. If they cannot find incorrect information, they should find other, unlisted sources that support information. Students will revise the Wikipedia entry to make it more detailed and accurate and add their own reliable sources to the document. The teacher is available to circulate and answer questions as needed.

Modification note: Students could handwrite their revisions if using or having enough computing devices is not possible. It is important for this activity to take place in class.

- Students will write reflective journals on the process.
- The teacher will prepare another Explore activity to begin the next part of the unit.

## Reflection Methods

- Students will journal or do another reflective exercise (Google Form) on the choices they made in determining their sources and revisions.
- Students will share their thinking and lessons learned in class discussions.

## Materials

| **Facilities:** | **Equipment (non-tech):** | **Equipment (tech):** |
| --- | --- | --- |
| ■ classroom or computer lab | ■ printouts of Web sites if devices unavailable | ■ device to view flipped video lesson<br>■ device to access Internet sites |

# Writing Lesson Plan (Traditional Flip)

## ENGLISH AND ITALIAN SONNETS

**Topic:** Types of Poetry

**Grade Level:** 6–10

**Skill:** Writing English and Italian Sonnets

**Established Goals:** Common Core State Standards

*CCSS.ELA-Literacy.CCRA.R.5* Analyze the structure of texts, including how specific sentences, paragraphs, and larger portions of the text (e.g., a section, chapter, scene, or stanza) relate to each other and the whole.

*CCSS.ELA-Literacy.CCRA.W.4* Produce clear and coherent writing in which the development, organization, and style are appropriate to task, purpose, and audience.

## Essential Question

How does the form and structure of a sonnet contribute to its meaning?

## Objectives

| *Students will understand . . .* | *Students will know . . .* | *Students will . . .* |
|---|---|---|
| ■ poems have different patterns that contribute to their form. | ■ structure of an English sonnet and Italian sonnet. | ■ be able to write accurate sonnets and evaluate how the form contributes to sonnets' meaning. |

## Assessment Evidence

### Performance Tasks:

- Students will write an accurate Italian sonnet and English sonnet with minimal scaffolding.

### Self-Assessments:

- The questions students ask will be used to evaluate their level of understanding as the unit progresses.

### Other Evidence:

- Students' final work.

## Learning Plan

*Lesson is based on 40-minute class periods but can be modified to fit your needs.*

**Flip:** Video introducing sonnets and explaining the pattern for English and Italian sonnets.

### Day 1:

- Provide students examples of English and Italian sonnets they read on their own at their pace/discretion. Answer any immediate questions.
- Students begin writing sonnets together in groups.
- The teacher circulates and is available to answer questions.

**Flip:** Video explaining how form contributes to meaning in a sonnet.

### Day 2:

- Students will answer questions in a Google Form designed to show reflection.
- Students begin to write sonnets on their own.
- The teacher circulates and is available to answer questions.

At the teacher's discretion, this lesson could be divided into two lessons for each type of poem.

## Reflection Methods

- Students will do a reflective exercise (Google Form) after watching the videos.
- Students will share their thinking about the poem and lessons learned in class discussions.
- Students will peer evaluate other students' poems.

## Materials

| Facilities: | Equipment (non-tech): | Equipment (tech): |
|---|---|---|
| ■ classroom or computer lab | ■ printouts of sample poems | ■ device to view flipped video lesson<br>■ device to access Internet sites |

## Student Sample

### Group Poem during Lesson

By Annie and Sylvia, seventh grade
A terrible British band
Was hated much
Because they had an ugly hand
They were not touched
And they were in the Americans' land
They ate a British lunch
That was all canned
They were a bad bunch
No one liked them
And one of them died
So there was nine of ten
People who liked them lied
There were practically none
They were no fun

### Individual Poem after Lesson

By Annie, seventh grade
The bright blue sky
With rolling clouds
With the wind very dry
And the yelling of crowds
Voices loud and clearIn the sunlit rays
Yelling various cheers
In their own craze
The wild wind
Making leaves fall down
Making the world destined
For the next season around
Everyone is yelling
The sky is compelling

# Writing Lesson Plan (Explore-Flip-Apply)

## ENGLISH AND ITALIAN SONNETS

Note: I took the group poem writing exercise out of this lesson and replaced it with another activity. If you liked the group writing activity, it could replace the Explore phase activity in this lesson.

**Topic:** Types of Poetry

**Grade Level:** 6–12

**Skill:** Writing English and Italian Sonnets

**Established Goals:** Common Core State Standards

*CCSS.ELA-Literacy.CCRA.R.5* Analyze the structure of texts, including how specific sentences, paragraphs, and larger portions of the text (e.g., a section, chapter, scene, or stanza) relate to each other and the whole.

*CCSS.ELA-Literacy.CCRA.W.4* Produce clear and coherent writing in which the development, organization, and style are appropriate to task, purpose, and audience.

## Essential Question

How does the form and structure of a sonnet contribute to its meaning?

## Objectives

| *Students will understand . . .* | *Students will know . . .* | *Students will . . .* |
|---|---|---|
| ■ poems have different patterns that contribute to their form. | ■ structure of an English sonnet and Italian sonnet. | ■ be able to write accurate sonnets and evaluate how the form contributes to their meaning. |

## Assessment Evidence

### Performance Tasks:

- Students will write an accurate Italian sonnet and English sonnet with minimal scaffolding.

### Self-Assessments:

- Students' questions will be used to evaluate their level of understanding as the unit progresses.

### Other Evidence:

- Students' final work.

## Learning Plan

*Lesson is based on 40-minute class periods but can be modified to meet your needs.*

### Day 1: Explore

- Give students three poems that are all Italian sonnets, but do not tell them what type of poems they are.

   Example poems: "Number 134" and "Sonnet 292" by Francis Petrarch and "On His Blindness" by John Milton.

- In small groups, students will analyze the poems' structure and determine the similarities and differences.
- The teacher explains to students these are all the same type of poem, so there will be similarities.
- Shuffle the groups and let different group members share the patterns their previous group recognized.
- At the end of the class, have groups present informally what they believe are the similarities.
- If students are close, advance them to the flip stage. If they are not, start again with more guidance from the teacher.

**Flip:** Video defining an Italian sonnet and giving the guidelines for an Italian sonnet. May also be used as a reminder of poetry terms such as feet, meter, and so forth.

### Day 2: Explore

- Provide another example of an Italian sonnet and/or have a quiz on Italian sonnets to check for understanding.
- Introduce examples of English sonnets for a similar exercise.

Examples: "Sonnet 1," "Sonnet 29," and "Sonnet 73" by Shakespeare.

- In small groups, students will compare new example poems to current understanding of Italian sonnets.
- Mix groups up and continue discussion.
- At the end of the class, have groups present informally what they believe are the similarities.

**Flip:** Video explaining what an English sonnet is and giving the guidelines for an English sonnet. May also be used as a reminder of poetry terms such as feet, meter, and so forth.

## Day 3: Explore

- Individually or in groups, students take one or two examples of sonnets and free write an answer to the question: how does the form of the sonnet contribute to its meaning?
- The teacher is available to circulate and answer questions.
- Students share some of their ideas as a group.

**Flip:** Video guiding students to see the way form can contribute to meaning.

## Day 4: Apply

- Students begin writing their own original sonnets.

  The teacher is available to circulate and answer questions.

## Reflection Methods

- Students will do a reflective exercise (Google Form) after watching the videos.
- Students will share their thinking about the poem and lessons learned in class discussions.
- Students will peer evaluate other students' poems using a method and criteria determined by the teacher in an earlier lesson.

## Materials

### Facilities:

- classroom or computer lab

### Equipment (non-tech):

- printouts of sample poems

### Equipment (tech):

- device to view flipped video lesson
- device to access Internet sites

## Student Sample

### Individual English Sonnet after Lesson

By Moira, seventh grade
The flower was so soft and gentle in the wind.
The petals will sway in the breeze and seem to shake.
The flower's stem will give a slight bend.
The flower is dainty but strong and can never break.
Branches can break, and leaves can fall,
Yet the beautiful sight is very strong.
Its strength and beauty will stand tall.
This is the place the flower will belong.
They say beauty is in the eye of the beholder,
Yet the flower has a beauty burns like fire.
A simple flame, to bright fire, to a small little smolder.
Everything is up tall and reaching higher.
The flower has qualities that make it tower,
But it is just a small dainty flower.

### Individual Italian Sonnet after Lesson

By Moira, seventh grade
I missed the moments when we were all fine.
Everyone got mad when we messed up everything.
No one would care to laugh, be happy or sing.
I miss when all of these moments were mine.
I remember back to these moments all the time.
I never thought of all the bad that one mistake could bring.
Just one small mistake, that one bad something.
How everything I had would be on the line.
Still I remember, mistakes can be fixed.
People can have happiness once again.
If you just try best, nothing bad can stay.
So I had good and bad finally mixed.
I just needed the right who, how and when.
And everything good could finally not stray.

# Writing Lesson Plan (Traditional Flip)

## ARGUMENT IN THE REAL WORLD

**Topic:** Argument Writing

**Grade Level:** 7–12

**Skill:** Using Argument in Writing

**Established Goals:** Common Core State Standards

*CCSS.ELA-Literacy.CCRA.W.1* Write arguments to support claims in an analysis of substantive topics or texts using valid reasoning and relevant and sufficient evidence.

*CCSS.ELA-Literacy.CCRA.W.2* Write informative/explanatory texts to examine and convey complex ideas and information clearly and accurately through the effective selection, organization, and analysis of content.

*CCSS.ELA-Literacy.CCRA.W.4* Produce clear and coherent writing in which the development, organization, and style are appropriate to task, purpose, and audience.

*CCSS.ELA-Literacy.CCRA.W.5* Develop and strengthen writing as needed by planning, revising, editing, rewriting, or trying a new approach.

*CCSS.ELA-Literacy.CCRA.W.6* Use technology, including the Internet, to produce and publish writing and to interact and collaborate with others.

## Essential Question

What are the necessary elements for effective argumentation in writing?

## Objectives

| Students will understand . . . | Students will know . . . | Students will . . . |
|---|---|---|
| ■ argument writing comes in many forms and has common elements in all forms. | ■ the elements of an effective argument. | ■ understand elements of an argument and be able to write an effective argument. |

## Assessment Evidence

| Performance Tasks: | Self-Assessments: | Other Evidence: |
|---|---|---|
| ■ Students will write an academic-level work that contains multiple elements of argument writing. | ■ Evaluate choices students make in selecting argument assignment. | ■ Students' final work. |

## Learning Plan

*Lesson is based on 40-minute class periods but can be modified to meet your needs.*

**Flip:** Video explaining what argument is and how to write an argument.

**Day 1:**

- Quick check for understanding using reflection form or student notes.
- Provide or have students find examples of argument writing (debates, etc.).
- The teacher is available to circulate and answer questions.

**Flip:** Video giving more guidance on argument writing.

**Day 2:**

- Students begin generating ideas for a writing assignment.
- Students then write an argument essay.

Alternate Assessment: Students could choose what type of argument writing they want to complete on an individual basis.

The teacher is available to circulate and answer questions.

## Reflection Methods

- Students will do a reflective exercise (Google Form) after watching the videos.
- Students will share their thinking about argument and lessons learned in class discussions.
- Students will peer evaluate other students' argument writing.

## Materials

### Facilities:

- classroom or computer lab

### Equipment (non-tech):

- printouts of argument examples

### Equipment (tech):

- device to view flipped video lesson
- device to access Internet sites

# Writing Lesson Plan (Explore-Flip-Apply)

## SHOULD MR. SMITH FLIP HIS CLASS?

**Topic:** Expository Writing

**Grade Level:** 7–12

**Skill:** Using Argument in Writing

**Established Goals:** Common Core State Standards

*CCSS.ELA-Literacy.CCRA.W.1* Write arguments to support claims in an analysis of substantive topics or texts using valid reasoning and relevant and sufficient evidence.

*CCSS.ELA-Literacy.CCRA.W.2* Write informative/explanatory texts to examine and convey complex ideas and information clearly and accurately through the effective selection, organization, and analysis of content.

*CCSS.ELA-Literacy.CCRA.W.4* Produce clear and coherent writing in which the development, organization, and style are appropriate to task, purpose, and audience.

*CCSS.ELA-Literacy.CCRA.W.5* Develop and strengthen writing as needed by planning, revising, editing, rewriting, or trying a new approach.

*CCSS.ELA-Literacy.CCRA.W.6* Use technology, including the Internet, to produce and publish writing and to interact and collaborate with others.

## Essential Question

What are the necessary elements for effective argument in writing?

## Objectives

| *Students will understand . . .* | *Students will know . . .* | *Students will . . .* |
|---|---|---|
| ■ argument writing comes in many forms and has common elements in all forms. | ■ the elements of an effective argument. | ■ understand elements of argument writing and be able to write an effective argument. |

## Assessment Evidence

| **Performance Tasks:** | **Self–Assessments:** | **Other Evidence:** |
|---|---|---|
| ■ Students will write an academic–level work that contains multiple elements of argument writing. | ■ Evaluate choices students make in selecting an argument assignment. | ■ Students' final work. |

## Learning Plan

*Lesson is based on 40-minute class periods but can be modified to suit your needs.*

Driving Question: What are the elements of effective argument writing?

### Day 1: Explore

- The teacher presents the students with a problem that has two sides and that would require a good argument, but does not tell the students that is the solution.

One example I use follows this script:

> "Mr. Smith in the Science Department is thinking of flipping his classroom similar to what I do. He wants your opinions on whether he should do it or not and he wants us to write it down so he can review it. What do you think we should say to him?"

- Short group discussion of some ideas.
- Students write individual letters to Mr. Smith explaining their position.
- As a group, student share their ideas.

## Day 2:

- Continue to share ideas and encourage them to debate their reasoning.
- The teacher guides the discussion toward the Driving Question.
- Group students by similar opinion and have them discuss their most effective arguments.

**Flip:** Video explaining what argument writing is and how arguments are selected and structured to be effective.

## Day 3: Explore

- Students revise their individual letters to Mr. Smith then make an effective argument for one side.
- The teacher is available to circulate and answer questions.
- Time allowed at teacher discretion. This is a practice activity.

**Flip:** Video giving more direction based on students' misconceptions and struggles in the practice exercise.

## Day 4: Apply

- Students begin writing an argument essay or alternate form of argument.

  The teacher is available to circulate and answer questions.

## Reflection Methods

- Students will do a reflective exercise (Google Form) after watching the videos.
- Students will share their thinking about argument writing and lessons learned in class discussions.
- Students will peer evaluate other students' argument work.

## Materials

| **Facilities:** | **Equipment (non-tech):** | **Equipment (tech):** |
| --- | --- | --- |
| ■ classroom or computer lab | ■ printouts of argument examples | ■ device to view flipped video lesson |
|  |  | ■ device to access Internet sites |

## Writing Lesson Plan

### AT THE RACES: WRITING OPEN-ENDED RESPONSES ON STANDARDIZED TESTS

*The following lesson was provided by Kate Baker, high school English teacher from Mana-hawkin, New Jersey.*

**Topic:** Writing Skills, Reading Skills

**Grade Level:** 9–10

**Skill:** Applying a strategy for writing open-ended responses on standardized tests

**Established Goals:** Common Core State Standards

*CCSS.ELA-Literacy.W.9–10.1* Write arguments to support claims in an analysis of substantive topics or texts, using valid reasoning and relevant and sufficient evidence.

*CCSS.ELA-Literacy.W.9–10.1d* Establish and maintain a formal style and objective tone while attending to the norms and conventions of the discipline in which they are writing.

*CCSS.ELA-Literacy.W.9–10.2* Write informative/explanatory texts to examine and convey complex ideas, concepts, and information clearly and accurately through the effective selection, organization, and analysis of content.

*CCSS.ELA-Literacy.W.9–10.4* Produce clear and coherent writing in which the development, organization, and style are appropriate to task, purpose, and audience. (Grade-specific expectations for writing types are defined in standards 1–3 above.)

*CCSS.ELA-Literacy.W.9–10.5* Develop and strengthen writing as needed by planning, revising, editing, rewriting, or trying a new approach, focusing on addressing what is most significant for a specific purpose and audience.

*CCSS.ELA-Literacy.W.9–10.8* Gather relevant information from multiple authoritative print and digital sources, using advanced searches effectively; assess the usefulness of each source in answering the research question; integrate information into the text selectively to maintain the flow of ideas, avoiding plagiarism and following a standard format for citation.

*CCSS.ELA-Literacy.W.9–10.10* Write routinely over extended time frames (time for research, reflection, and revision) and shorter time frames (a single sitting or a day or two) for a range of tasks, purposes, and audiences.

## Essential Question

How can textual evidence and connections be used to write a high-scoring open-ended response?

## Objectives

| *Students will understand . . .* | *Students will know . . .* | *Students will . . .* |
|---|---|---|
| ■ all writing follows a similar structure. | ■ how to write an open-ended response following a specific structure. | ■ write open-ended responses;<br>■ evaluate classmates' responses. |

## Assessment Evidence

| **Performance Tasks:** | **Self-Assessments:** | **Other Evidence:** |
|---|---|---|
| ■ Students will demonstrate understanding and application of RACES strategy. | ■ Google Forms<br>■ Class discussion<br>■ Written responses | ■ Edmodo posts<br>■ Students' scores on open-ended responses |

## Learning Plan

■ Previous to flipping, I introduced my students to testing strategies that align with New Jersey's HSPA standardized test via a PowerPoint presentation on how to mark up prompts and questions using the Circle & RUN strategy and an additional PowerPoint on how to write an open-ended response using the RACES strategy. The students copy down the notes on the strategy, then write numerous practice responses until students demonstrate mastery of the strategy. Throughout the year, students write responses in context with the literature studied to reinforce the skills and maintain proficiency.

**Flip:** Using a flipped approach for introducing and initial practicing of HSPA skills, activities were group and inquiry oriented. Students became detectives figuring out the meaning of the strategies and how to apply them.

- At home, students viewed a short video posted on Edmodo on the Circle & RUN strategy (http://youtu.be/cpjrS6JTORg). I used a PowerPoint I had and made a screencast using Screencast-O-Matic. Students took notes on the video and marked up practice questions that I checked the next day.

The next day in class, students sat in groups of their choosing. They were given a paper copy of the RACES PowerPoint presentation (http://tinyurl.com/mqkslzy) instead of listening to me lecture. Students were also given a sample scored open-ended question (http://tinyurl.com/lora6qm) with multiple sample scored answers that aligned with steps on the rubric. All papers were hole punched for inclusion in their three-ring binders. I gave general directions (*"Figure out the meaning of this 'stuff' and what are you supposed to do."*) and while students worked, I circulated around the group *asking* guiding questions as needed. Any of their questions were answered with an additional question from me. I did not give them answers.

- Next day in class, I gave them an open-ended question and with minimal directions said: use your resources to answer the question and earn a score of four on the rubric. Student responses were not collected.
- Next day in class, and still in groups, students revised a sample answer. Students then self-assessed their own open-ended responses and made any changes needed.
- Students engaged in structured peer editing and evaluated each other's open-ended responses using Google Forms.
- Evaluators filled out a form assessing the writer's response (http://tinyurl.com/oqsa5jo), and a copy of the evaluation was automatically sent to the writer via the autocrat script. I maintained a master list of evaluations.
- Writers reviewed the response and filled out a form assessing the evaluators' scoring (see an example at http://tinyurl.com/kpeckdw) and reflecting on this process; a copy of the reflection was sent automatically to the evaluator via the autocrat script. I kept a master list.
- Disagreements with scores will be addressed in a writers' conference moderated by me.

## Reflection Methods

- Students will self-evaluate and peer evaluate their responses.
- Students will share their thinking through group and class discussion and Edmodo posts.

## Materials

| Facilities: | Equipment (non-tech): | Equipment (tech): |
|---|---|---|
| classroom | paper copies of New Jersey HSPA rubric, sample OE responses, RACES strategy | device to view flipped video lesson |
| | | device to access open-ended response |

## Student Sample

Sample student question: The stories about the Trojan War showcase many characters, both mortal and immortal, whose actions helped the Greeks defeat the Trojans. In your opinion, who was most responsible for helping the Greeks win the war (or who was most responsible for the Trojans losing the war)? Why? Include specific information to show that you have thought seriously about this topic. (The question can also be found online: http://tinyurl.com/k5k2vpy.)

As you may have noticed, Explore–Flip–Apply lessons can sometimes take longer than a Traditional Flip. However, they are more inquiry based, so your students may move faster or slower than anticipated. The lessons require more teacher discretion on when to move forward and what content to put in the videos. Some of the activities are the same in both models, but the introduction to the lesson and placement of the video instruction is different. Because flipping is student centered, it is important to allow room in your plan for students to raise questions and suggest ideas you might not anticipate. These lessons were all based around writing instruction. In the next chapter, the lessons focus on grammar instruction.

### Flipping Your Thoughts: Reflections on What You've Just Read

Which of these lessons are you eager to try? Why?

Do you see ways you can flip your own writing lessons?

What lessons of your own do you envision flipping?

Was writing instruction the first thing you thought you wanted to flip? Why or why not?

# Flipped Language Instruction

For some teachers, language skills (grammar and vocabulary) are the first content they flip, and, for others, language skills are the second. Either way, many find grammar and vocabulary easy subjects to flip. What I really love about using a flip to teach grammar and vocabulary is that I can have fun, engaging, and lively activities in class and don't need to spend a lot of time on grammar rules. The videos handle that. If the students forget, they can go back to watch the videos or look at their notes I have them take. The activities I use then rely heavily on peer instruction. Language instruction is a lot more enjoyable for my students and for me after I flipped.

## Language Lesson Plan

### COMMA USAGE

**Topic:** Grammar

**Grade Level:** 6–8

**Skill:** Comma Usage

**Established Goals:** Common Core State Standards

*CCSS.ELA-Literacy.L.6.2a* Use punctuation (commas, parentheses, dashes) to set off nonrestrictive/parenthetical elements.

*CCSS.ELA-Literacy.L.7.2a* Use a comma to separate coordinate adjectives.

*CCSS.ELA-Literacy.L.8.2a* Use punctuation (comma, ellipsis, dash) to indicate a pause or break.

## Essential Question

What difference does having proper comma usage make when writing?

## Objectives

| *Students will understand . . .* | *Students will know . . .* | *Students will . . .* |
|---|---|---|
| ■ comma usage, as with any mechanic, is important to writing. | ■ the 11 basic rules of comma usage. | ■ identify proper comma placement across multiple texts. |

## Assessment Evidence

### Performance Tasks:

- Students will place commas in a non-punctuated paragraph or sentence.
- Students will discuss why the placement was chosen.

### Self-Assessments:

- Students' writing samples showing proper or improper comma usage.

### Other Evidence:

- Students' general writing portfolios.

## Learning Plan

*Lesson is based on 40-minute class periods but can be modified to meet your needs.*

**Flip:** Students watch a short video discussing the rules of comma usage. I ask them to take detailed notes on the rules. I also ask them to reflect on rules they didn't already know or rules about which they may be unclear.

### Day 1:

- I like to start the class with this quote from Lynne Truss (2003) in *Eats, Shoots & Leaves:* "The rule is: don't use commas like a stupid person. I mean it. More than any other mark, the comma requires the writer to use intelligent discretion and to be simply alert to potential ambiguity."
- As a class, we briefly discuss the quote.
- Next, I post on the board or interactive whiteboard a paragraph from a mentor text. If you struggle to find good mentor texts, look to Jeff Anderson's *Mechanically Inclined* (2005). The mentor text posted has no punctuation.
- As a group, we quickly fill in the periods. My students are good at finding those, so we don't spend a lot of time on this.
- Next, I have them write the paragraph down and punctuate any commas they believe should be in the paragraph. I also have them total the number of commas.
- I then ask for a show of hands for the different number of commas. If it is a difficult text, there may be a variety of answers (that's ideal). If it is too simple of a text, you'll have a lot of common answers.
- I then ask the students to pair themselves with other students who had a different total number of commas than they had.
- Next, the students discuss each comma they placed and why. At the end of their discussion, they should have reached a consensus on the number of commas in the text.

- I again ask the students how many commas they came up with and compare that variety of numbers to the previous. Ideally, more students should have the same number of commas than before.
- We discuss which commas they talked about the most. However, I still don't give them the correct answers.
- I ask them to review the comma rules again for the next class.

**Flip:** Potentially, another video may be needed here depending on how accurate the students were in their comma usage. This video would focus on the comma rules students struggled to understand.

## Day 2:

- I ask the students to search for the mentor text online and see if they can find the correct comma usage.
- Again, we discuss problem commas as a group and try to come to a consensus as to why each comma is placed.
- I wrap the discussion by giving them the correct answers and the correct reasons and determine if further instruction will be needed.

## Reflection Methods

- Students will do a reflective exercise (Google Form) after watching the videos.
- Students will share their thinking about comma usage and lessons learned in class discussions.
- Students use peer instruction with classmates on comma usage.

## Materials

| Facilities: | Equipment (non-tech): | Equipment (tech): |
|---|---|---|
| - classroom or computer lab | - n/a | - device to view flipped video lesson<br>- device to access Internet sites |

## Sample Mentor Text

Choosing a mentor text can be a time-consuming process, but it is critical to the effectiveness of this unit. Quite often, I use this example titled "My Father's Summers" by Kathi Appelt found in Jeff Anderson's text (2005):

"What I wasn't used to was having his smell back, the smoke from his Camel cigarettes, his Old Spice aftershave, the shoe polish he used on his boots. All those father odors, filling up the house. My mother opened every window, waxed the wood furniture, sprayed room freshener in every corner. She scrubbed the tiles on the bathroom floor, scrubbed the dog's water bowl, scrubbed her hair, her hands, her face, shiny. Then she sat in her convertible and wept it all away, all but the smell. I can't scrub the air," she said. And so he was there, but not really. Where was he?"

However, Troy Hicks (2013) asserts that good mentor texts are all around us in digital writing examples. Teachers should encourage students to find their own digital texts in media that interest them. An extension activity on this lesson could be to have students search for appropriate digital texts.

If your students are like mine, determining the difference between gerunds, participles, and infinitives can be challenging. Depending on the level of your students, they may have not had any exposure to these verbal phrases. If that is the case, an exploratory activity can be a real struggle. In that instance, I would start with an introduction video and follow up with more focused videos as the students progress. If they have some experience, you may not need to start with a content video, but rather have them explore previous knowledge first.

# Language Lesson Plan

## VERBAL PHRASES: GERUNDS, PARTICIPLES, INFINITIVES

**Topic:** Grammar

**Grade Level:** 7–12

**Skill:** Verbal Phrases

**Established Goals:** Common Core Standards

*CCSS.ELA-Literacy.L.7.1a* Explain the function of phrases and clauses in general and their function in specific sentences.

*CCSS.ELA-Literacy.L.8.1a* Explain the function of verbals (gerunds, participles, infinitives) in general and their function in particular sentences.

*CCSS.ELA-Literacy.L.9–10.1b* Use various types of phrases (noun, verb, adjectival, adverbial, participial, prepositional, absolute) and clauses (independent, dependent, noun, relative, adverbial) to convey specific meanings and add variety and interest to writing or presentations.

## Essential Question

What clues will help us identify the differences in verbal phrases?

## Objectives

| *Students will understand . . .* | *Students will know . . .* | *Students will . . .* |
|---|---|---|
| ■ how verbal phrases are used. | ■ the definition of each type of verbal phrase. | ■ identify the differences between verbal phrases correctly. |

## Assessment Evidence

### Performance Tasks:

- Students will identify examples of each type of verbal phrase.
- Students will write their own examples of each type of verbal phase.

### Self-Assessments:

- Class discussion and individual conferences.

### Other Evidence:

- Students' general writing portfolios.

## Learning Plan

*Lesson is based on 40-minute class periods but can be modified to meet your needs.*

**Flip:** Students watch a video defining the three verbal phrases we plan to cover: gerund, participle, and infinitive.

### Day 1:

- Students are divided into small groups of three members each. They are asked to find an example of each type of verbal phrase. Each member of the group should be able to explain why each example is correct. My students know Purdue's Online Writing Lab (owl.english.purdue.edu/owl) well and many would go there. Or they would do a Google search and take the first example that comes up. I make the rule that if their example is the same as one other group's, they have to return to their group and find another example. Students usually search a little harder for examples to avoid doing the exercise twice.
- Groups then divide up and mix into different groups of three. Each member of the new group shares three examples and explains the reasons. I would be circulating this whole time and listening to the discussions. At this point, I may open up for some group discussion and determine if more instruction is needed.

**Flip:** If more instruction is needed, students will watch a video explaining the uses of the verbal phrases and some tips to help identify them.

### Day 2:

- Students get into groups of three again and this time write examples of verbal phrases in complex sentences. They cannot use the examples from the previous activity, nor can they just replace a different word into the same sentence.

- Students then shuffle their groups and discuss their examples as in the previous activity.

At this point, I determine if more instruction is needed or I may give them a quiz to assess understanding. More individualized instruction may be needed for some of the students at this time.

## Reflection Methods

- Students will do a reflective exercise (Google Form) on verbal phrases after watching the videos.
- Students will share their thinking about verbal phrases and lessons learned in class discussions.
- Students use peer instruction with classmates on verbal phrases.

## Materials

| Facilities: | Equipment (non-tech): | Equipment (tech): |
|---|---|---|
| ■ classroom or computer lab | ■ n/a | ■ device to view flipped video lesson<br>■ device to access Internet sites |

Our ultimate goal is that our students use proper grammar and mechanics in their writing. So, often I try to combine grammar exercises with writing tasks. The following lesson uses the students' own writing and the writing of their peers to determine levels of understanding in certain areas. I combine the following lessons with identifying parts of speech, but they could be combined with identifying parts of sentences, clauses, phrases, and more.

# Language Lesson Plan

## PARTS OF SPEECH

**Topic:** Grammar

**Grade Level:** 5–12

**Skill:** Identifying Parts of Speech

**Established Goals:** Common Core State Standards

*CCSS.ELA-Literacy.L.7.3* Use knowledge of language and its conventions when writing, speaking, reading, or listening.

*CCSS.ELA-Literacy.L.8.1* Demonstrate command of the conventions of standard English grammar and usage when writing or speaking.

*CCSS.ELA-Literacy.L.9–10.1b* Use various types of phrases (noun, verb, adjectival, adverbial, participial, prepositional, absolute) and clauses (independent, dependent, noun, relative, adverbial) to convey specific meanings and add variety and interest to writing or presentations.

*CCSS.ELA-Literacy.L.11–12.3* Apply knowledge of language to understand how language functions in different contexts, to make effective choices for meaning or style, and to comprehend more fully when reading or listening.

## Essential Question

Why does variety in our uses of the eight parts of speech matter?

## Objectives

| *Students will understand . . .* | *Students will know . . .* | *Students will . . .* |
|---|---|---|
| ■ the parts of speech get more in depth each year. | ■ the eight parts of speech. | ■ identify the parts of speech in use. |

## Assessment Evidence

| **Performance Tasks:** | **Self-Assessments:** | **Other Evidence:** |
|---|---|---|
| ▪ Students will identify examples of each part of speech in their writing and their peers' writing.<br>▪ Students will examine their uses of the different parts of speech and revise their work to improve. | ▪ Class discussion and individual conferences. | ▪ Students' general writing portfolios. |

## Learning Plan

*Lesson is based on 40-minute class periods but can be modified to meet your needs.*

**Flip:** Students watch a video reviewing the eight parts of speech. Depending on the level of the students, the video could be more complex if they have a solid understanding of the basic parts of speech.

### Day 1:

- Students will review another student's page of writing. The writing should be something they are currently working on for class or something recently completed.
- The students will use sets of colored highlighters, markers, colored pencils, or, in Google Docs, the background color highlighting feature. Using the different colors, students should make a key. For instance, blue means noun, red means verb, and so forth. The students should go through their peers' writing samples and highlight or underline based on their color coding every part of speech they find.
- The teacher should circulate and answer questions. Depending on the level of the students, this could take the entire period.
- Toward the end of the activity, students pinpoint as a group which words they struggled with identifying. The teacher can write some on the board, looking for trends in student understanding. For example, my students consistently forget that an article is an adjective. So, if several students had left articles unhighlighted, I know more instruction in those areas is needed.

**Flip:** If more instruction is needed, students will watch a video explaining the uses of the parts of speech to help identify them.

## Day 2:

- Students would then take their own writing and do the same exercise. The goal of this is to highlight every part of speech on the page.
- A good follow-up exercise is to have them get percentages on how many nouns versus verbs they used and so forth. Computer programs and Web sites are available that can do this for them, but it is a good exercise for them to do on their own as well.

Students should use this exercise to add more variety to their writing and revise the sample work used.

## Reflection Methods

- Students will do a reflective exercise (Google Form) on parts of speech after watching the videos.
- Students will share their thinking about the parts of speech and lessons learned in class discussions.

## Materials

| **Facilities:** | **Equipment (non-tech):** | **Equipment (tech):** |
|---|---|---|
| ■ classroom or computer lab | ■ printouts of student work | ■ device to view flipped video lesson <br> ■ device to access Internet sites |

# Language Lesson Plan

## ASK THE EXPERT

**Topic:** Language: Vocabulary

**Grade Level:** 5–12

**Skill:** Vocabulary Review

**Established Goals:** Common Core State Standards

*CCSS.ELA-Literacy.CCRA.L.4* Determine or clarify the meaning of unknown and multiple-meaning words and phrases by using context clues, analyzing meaningful word parts, and consulting general and specialized reference materials as appropriate.

*CCSS.ELA-Literacy.CCRA.L.5* Demonstrate understanding of figurative language, word relationships, and nuances in word meanings.

*CCSS.ELA-Literacy.CCRA.L.6* Acquire and use accurately a range of general academic and domain-specific words and phrases sufficient for reading, writing, speaking, and listening at the college and career readiness level; demonstrate independence in gathering vocabulary knowledge when encountering an unknown term important to comprehension or expression.

## Essential Question

How can we use context clues, word parts, or general knowledge to construct the meaning of words?

## Objectives

| ***Students will understand . . .*** | ***Students will know . . .*** | ***Students will . . .*** |
|---|---|---|
| ■ words have certain constructs that can help determine meaning. | ■ the skills necessary for analyzing words and sentences to determine meaning. | ■ determine the meaning of words based on word parts, context clues, and general knowledge. |

## Assessment Evidence

| **Performance Tasks:** | **Self-Assessments:** | **Other Evidence:** |
|---|---|---|
| ■ Students will guess the meanings of unknown words.<br>■ Students will find the words in use.<br>■ Students will provide examples of the words in their own use. | ■ Students' use of vocabulary in writing. | ■ Students' overall improvement in writing and speaking in portfolio. |

## Learning Plan

Note: These activities may only take part of a class period depending on the time available and other assignments over the course of several days. Or, you could do intensive vocabulary mini-units if that works better in your schedule.

### Day 1:

- Students know the upcoming vocabulary unit, but haven't been asked to review it yet. Some may have started early, but most have not. Vocabulary units are based around word parts (we use Thompson's 2013 book *Word within the Word*) so students may have some knowledge to apply from previous units.
- The class plays an improv game called "Ask the Expert."
- I select three students to come to the front of the class. Around the room I've posted A, B, or C in three of the corners.
- I tell the three students one word from the upcoming vocabulary unit.
- Each student becomes an "expert" on that word and gives his or her definition of it. Some students will break the word into parts and try to figure it out; others will try to be the funniest. Either is fine.

- After the three students give their definitions, the students vote on which is correct by going to a specific corner (A, B, or C). I make note of how many were correct (if one of the answers was close to correct).
- I then give the students the correct definition.
- We continue this process until we are through most, if not all the words.

**Flip:** Students will watch a video of me giving the proper pronunciation and definition of each word, including using it in a sample sentence. Students take notes on the words, using either the book or my video.

## Day 2:

- Students are put into groups of two or three.
- Each group takes five words and, through an Internet search, finds each word in use somewhere in literature.
- Each group also writes an example sentence (not the one given in the video) of each of its five words.
- Group members then mix with other groups and share their examples. By the end of the class, each student should have notes of two examples (one in literature and one original) from every word in the unit.

The students review words on their own time.

## Day 3:

- The class plays "Ask the Expert" again.
- This time we vote anonymously so students can't vote based on what they see other students voting. I usually just do head down hands up, but a response system or poll anywhere text system could also be used. I am using this time to assess how many students are getting the words correct or not to determine if more instruction/practice is needed.

Once I determine enough instruction and practice has taken place a summative assessment is scheduled.

## Reflection Methods

Students will review their notes in preparation for further assessment.

## Materials

### Facilities:

- classroom

### Equipment (non-tech):

- Some way to quickly choose answers. In this case, letters posted on the wall.

### Equipment (tech):

- device to view flipped video lesson
- possible device for response system.

## Flipping Your Thoughts: Reflections on What You've Just Read

Are language skills an area you had thought about flipping?

Which of these lessons are you eager to try?

Do you have some lessons you could modify with a flip?

What lessons of your own do you envision flipping?

# Flipped Reading Instruction

Reading instruction is probably where I've seen the largest variety of flipping. Maybe that's because reading comprehension is an intangible skill that is done mostly in the students' heads, and finding ways to accurately assess such skills can be difficult.

I've also heard many teachers make the statement, "English teachers have flipped for years. They have students read at home and then they discuss in class." I am bothered by that assertion because I believe it doesn't fit the core basis of what defines a Flipped Classroom.

First, reading at home is usually not a lower-level processing skill. In a flipped environment, teachers offload material covering lower-level processing skills and place it in a technology that can be consumed at a time and place of the students' choosing. Unless my students are reading purely for entertainment value, they need to process what they are reading using reading comprehension skills and making connections to previously learned content. In other words, they should be applying what they've learned at this point, not simply consuming information. If they are unable to do this, I need to assess why that is and how we can fix that, which is difficult if they are reading at home.

Second, discussion isn't individualized instruction. As teachers, we use discussion to create connections and deeper thought on a topic. I think we've all had students who are very good at manipulating the "system" to make it look like they comprehended the reading, whether they are mimicking others' comments, talking a lot on the easy questions so they can avoid being called on for other questions, or reading SparkNotes right before class to get enough of an understanding to talk their way through it. And the students who clearly aren't getting it aren't getting the one-on-one attention that would be helpful for them. If some content is not understood by the group and the teacher must derail the discussion for a lesson, that usually becomes direct instruction. I'm not saying that I'm against it and we should never do whole group discussion. There are benefits to teacher-led discussion in a Flipped Classroom and I am not underestimating that (Moran & Young, in press). I'm just saying the discussion element in itself is not what makes a classroom flipped.

Here's an example: I use *Lord of the Flies* to teach about symbolism, among other things. I send my kids home to read and then we discuss the symbolism in class. What if my students don't know the definition of symbolism? Then I need an instructional step, maybe a video, to explain it. Now, they know the definition; I still can't just send them out to read because, as we all know, knowing the definition and understanding what symbolism is does not mean a student can identify it. I believe I need to get my students to at least the identifying stage before I can comfortably send them home to read on their own. Then, class time can be used for analyzing and evaluating the symbolism. If I can't get them to those higher-level stages in class with me, then simply reading at home is not a productive use of their time.

I am not, however, postulating that students spend all their time reading in class either. I believe there needs to be a blending of reading at home and reading at school. Students should be able to read independently while at the same time getting opportunities to ask questions of their teachers or their peers. Teachers who use online discussion tools like blogs and wikis have the same ideas. Reading and understanding literature and nonfiction text is a great opportunity for teachers to expand their students' learning beyond the classroom walls. Admittedly, adding a flip into that learning takes some creativity on the teachers' part, and it may not seem blatantly evident when you initially start your Flipped Classroom.

The first lesson here is the example I used earlier of *Lord of the Flies* by William Golding. Tap into that understanding of symbolism by using a flip.

# Reading Lesson Plan

## SYMBOLISM IN *LORD OF THE FLIES*

**Topic:** Reading Skills

**Grade Level:** 8–12

**Skill:** Identifying Symbolism in Literature

**Established Goals:** Common Core State Standards

*CCSS.ELA-Literacy.RL.8.9* Analyze how a modern work of fiction draws on themes, patterns of events, or character types from myths, traditional stories, or religious works such as the Bible, including describing how the material is rendered new.

*CCSS.ELA-Literacy.RL.9–10.1* Cite strong and thorough textual evidence to support analysis of what the text says explicitly as well as inferences drawn from the text.

*CCSS.ELA-Literacy.RL.11–12.1* Cite strong and thorough textual evidence to support analysis of what the text says explicitly as well as inferences drawn from the text, including determining where the text leaves matters uncertain.

## Essential Question

How does symbolism enhance the theme or main idea of a novel?

## Objectives

| *Students will understand . . .* | *Students will know . . .* | *Students will . . .* |
|---|---|---|
| ■ the importance of identifying symbolism as it relates to meaning. | ■ the definition of symbolism. | ■ identify symbolism in a novel with age-appropriate text complexity. |

## Assessment Evidence

**Performance Tasks:**

- Students will identify examples of symbolism individually in reflection.
- Students will identify symbolism in group discussions.

**Self-Assessments:**

- Class discussion and individual reflection analysis.

**Other Evidence:**

- Students' general understanding of the entire text based off their understanding of symbolism.

## Learning Plan

**Flip:** Students watch a pre-reading video defining symbolism.

When reading:

- I let the students know when they reach a particular point in the book to stop reading and watch a video. For instance, when they reach this quote in *Lord of the Flies,* "We've got to have rules and obey them. After all, we're not savages," I ask them to watch a video.

**Flip:** In the video, I explain that this is one example of symbolism. I give them a reflection form to fill in and ask them what that quote might symbolize. I also ask them to try and identify another example of symbolism near that example.

- Once I've reviewed the reflections, we have a group discussion on symbolism. After the discussion, they will read in class or do another exercise in identifying symbolism and I can circulate to have conversations with students who didn't do well on the reflection form.

**Flip:** If more instruction is needed, students watch a video directing them to another example of symbolism and we keep cycling back to it as necessary throughout the reading of the novel.

It is important that students do a lot of the identifying in class, whether through discussion or reflection forms, for accurate assessment purposes.

## Reflection Methods

- Students will do a reflective exercise (Google Form) on symbolism after watching the videos.
- Students will share their thinking through discussion and one-on-one conferences.

## Materials

### Facilities:

- classroom or computer lab

### Equipment (non–tech):

- text you are reading

### Equipment (tech):

- device to view flipped video lesson
- device to annotate text

# Reading Lesson Plan

## "MAGGY, MILLY, MOLLY, AND MAY"
## BY E.E. CUMMINGS

*This lesson was provided to me by Lisa Highfill from Pleasanton, California. At the time she used this lesson, she was a fifth grade teacher.*

**Topic:** Cycles of Learning–Flipped ELA–Poetry Analysis

**Grade Level:** 5

**Subject:** Reading Comprehension

**Established Goals:** Common Core State Standards

*CCSS.ELA-Literacy.RL.5.1* Quote accurately from a text when explaining what the text says explicitly and when drawing inferences from the text.

*CCSS.ELA-Literacy.RL.5.2* Determine a theme of a story, drama, or poem from details in the text, including how characters in a story or drama respond to challenges or how the speaker in a poem reflects on a topic; summarize the text.

*CCSS.ELA-Literacy.RL.5.3* Compare and contrast two or more characters, settings, or events in a story or drama, drawing on specific details in the text (e.g., how characters interact).

## Essential Question

How does your thinking change about a poem as you experience it in different ways?

## Objectives

| *Students will understand . . .* | *Students will know . . .* | *Students will . . .* |
|---|---|---|
| ■ written words can have multiple meanings when taken out of context. <br> ■ once text is back in context, the initial meaning changes. | ■ context means everything when interpreting or analyzing written text. <br> ■ written words are open to various interpretations. | ■ respond to a written prompt. <br> ■ analyze a poem. <br> ■ share their thinking clearly in writing. |

## Assessment Evidence

| **Performance Tasks:** | **Self-Assessments:** | **Other Evidence:** |
|---|---|---|
| ■ Students will read and analyze a line from a poem. <br> ■ Students will continue the analysis through a flipped lesson. <br> ■ Students will share their thinking during school lessons and on Padlet and a Google Form. <br> ■ Students will participate in the Explore-Explain-Apply cycle of learning. | ■ Class discussions will shed light on personal comprehension levels. <br> ■ Adjusted schema and thinking is the expectation as new insights are shared. | ■ Communication skills will improve in writing and speaking. <br> ■ Synthesis of the topic will be evident. <br> ■ New skills in poetry analysis will emerge. |

## Learning Plan

Inquiry Hook/Activity Procedure:

- **Explore (in class):** I show the students a picture and ask them to think about what it means. The picture can have a sea image of some sort and will have the words, "for whatever (like a you or a me) it's always ourselves we find in the sea."

- They will write their thinking in their writer's notebooks, then share with classmates and finally post their thinking on Padlet (see their example at http://padlet.com/wall/5oem79rit5).
- Next, I let the students know that this is just one line (the last line) to a famous poem by e.e. cummings, "maggy, milly, molly and may," and tonight they will learn about the rest of the poem in a flipped lesson.
- **Explain: (flipped at home)** Students learn about the entire poem by viewing an oral telling of it on YouTube (see their example at www.youtube.com/watch?v = PZ_06r0OGR4&feature = youtu.be).
- They will have the opportunity to view it with graphic representations (www.youtube.com/watch?v = L9vI7TVy-eE&feature = youtu.be) and a musical version (www.youtube.com/watch?v = ELMq2jzWyKo&feature = youtu.be) in order to experiment with aiding comprehension for various learning styles through the use of alternative modalities (visual, oral with no representations, or musical).
- Students will complete a Google Form to collect their thinking.
- **Apply: (in class)** Students will try the activity again in class by analyzing a poem "Blackbird" (written text only). They will share their thinking about the poem by writing their annotations on paper and sharing their thinking during Reader's Workshop.
- Next, I will play the song "Blackbird" by the Beatles for the class and watch for the "Aha!" moment to occur!
- Students will then share if or how their thinking has changed about the "poem" now that they realize and hear it as a song.
- Through inquiry, students will make the connection that all music is poetry, an art form that is open to interpretation.
- **Activity:** Students will next choose a song they love, find the lyrics, and post them on a Glogster. If available, they will post a video of the song or an audio file on the Glog. They will also post their interpretation of the song in a song in a text box on the Glog.
- Glogsters will be shared with classmates and others by embedding them on a Google site, and they will be tweeted out for others to enjoy.

## Reflection Methods

- Students will share their thinking about the process of poetry analysis during a class reflection time.
- Students will share their thinking about the poem and lessons learned in class discussions.
- Students will try the activity again using a variety of other pieces including songs such as "Blackbird" by the Beatles.

## Materials

**Facilities:**

- classroom meetings
- weekly computer lab

**Equipment (non–tech):**

- poem by e.e. cummings
- song—"Blackbird" by the Beatles

**Equipment (tech):**

- device to view flipped video lesson

## Student Sample

Explore and Explain Samples:

- The hook-Padlet activity (http://padlet.com/wall/5oem79rit5)
- The flipped lesson page (https://sites.google.com/site/highfillcrew1112/home/flipped-learning/poetry-analysis)
- Student responses to the form (http://tinyurl.com/mahl46o)

# Reading Lesson Plan

## DRAMA: THE THREE- AND FIVE-ACT PLAYS

**Topic:** Drama: The Three- and Five-Act Plays

**Grade Level:** 8–12

**Skill:** Identifying Structure of a Three-Act and a Five-Act Play

**Established Goals:** Common Core State Standards

*CCSS.ELA-Literacy.RL.6.3* Describe how a particular story or drama's plot unfolds in a series of episodes as well as how the characters respond or change as the plot moves toward a resolution.

*CCSS.ELA-Literacy.RL.7.3* Analyze how particular elements of a story or drama interact (e.g., how setting shapes the characters or plot).

*CCSS.ELA-Literacy.RL.7.5* Analyze how a drama or poem's form or structure (e.g., soliloquy, sonnet) contributes to its meaning.

*CCSS.ELA-Literacy.RL.7.6* Analyze how an author develops and contrasts the points of view of different characters or narrators in a text.

*CCSS.ELA-Literacy.RL.8.3* Analyze how particular lines of dialogue or incidents in a story or drama propel the action, reveal aspects of a character, or provoke a decision.

*CCSS.ELA-Literacy.RL.9–10.9* Analyze how an author draws on and transforms source material in a specific work (e.g., how Shakespeare treats a theme or topic from Ovid or the Bible or how a later author draws on a play by Shakespeare).

*CCSS.ELA-Literacy.RL.11–12.3* Analyze the impact of the author's choices regarding how to develop and relate elements of a story or drama (e.g., where a story is set, how the action is ordered, how the characters are introduced and developed).

## Essential Question

How does the structure of a play advance the plot?

## Objectives

| *Students will understand . . .* | *Students will know . . .* | *Students will . . .* |
|---|---|---|
| ■ a story needs to advance the plot. | ■ the structure of a story or play helps determine how to move the plot forward. | ■ identify a variety of play structures and compare them to plot structures. |

## Assessment Evidence

| **Performance Tasks:** | **Self-Assessments:** | **Other Evidence:** |
|---|---|---|
| ■ Students will improvise a play making choices to move through the three-act or five-act format. | ■ Class discussion and individual reflection analysis. | ■ Students' general understanding of the entire text based off their understanding of symbolism. |

## Learning Plan

- ■ I start with an improv game called "Choose Your Own Adventure." Two or three students improvise a scene. At various points, I freeze the scene and ask for three suggestions of where the scene should go next. The class then votes on where the actors go with the scene. I stop two or four times. If I want the play to be three acts, I stop it twice. If I want the play to be five acts, I stop it four times. However, I don't give students directions on what to do with the scene when I have stopped it. I want them making choices without my input.
- ■ After the game, the class has a discussion on the choices the actors made and why. At this point, students may or may not make a connection to the three-act or five-act play. Sometimes they will make a connection to plot structure. They normally realize they were making decisions to advance the story even if they didn't realize it at the time.

**Flip:** In the video, the definitions of a three-act and five-act play are given, as well as some historical background.

- Students return to class and we discuss the three-act and five-act play structure.
- We play the improv game again; this time I give them small amounts of guidance at each stop in the action. For instance, I might say, "This is now the second act; think about what would go into a second act."
- After we act out a three-act play, we discuss as a class if the actors made choices that followed the three-act play or not.
- We then improvise a five-act play, again with a little guidance from me and followed by a similar discussion.
- I attempt to get everyone involved through the course of the period as either actors or those giving choices to the actors. Then, during the discussion, I ask why they made certain choices (and "I don't know" isn't an acceptable answer). That way I can hear their thought process as it relates to the play's structure.
- We follow all this up with a reflection writing activity to check for understanding and then move into reading a three-act and/or five-act play.

Note: We have a small outdoor stage behind our school used for a variety of activities. Weather permitting, I take the kids to that stage and get them out of the classroom for these improv games. I recommend that, if you have a space for this outside the classroom, you use it. The change in location and the kinesthetic movement really helps add engagement to this lesson.

## Reflection Methods

- Students will do a reflective exercise (Google Form) on the structure of a three-act and five-act play after watching the videos.
- Students will share their thinking through discussion and one-on-one conferences.

## Materials

### Facilities:

- classroom or stage (if available)

### Equipment (non-tech):

- text you are reading

### Equipment (tech):

- device to view flipped video lesson

# Reading Lesson Plan

## OF MICE AND MEN: INTRODUCTORY IDIOMS

*The following lesson is courtesy of Kate Baker, high school English teacher from Manahawkin, New Jersey.*

**Topic:** Speaking Skills, Reading Skills

**Grade Level:** 9–10

**Skill:** Understanding Idioms of a Specific Context for Novel Study

**Established Goals:** Common Core State Standards

*CCSS.ELA-Literacy.SL.9–10.1* Initiate and participate effectively in a range of collaborative discussions (one on one, in groups, and teacher led) with diverse partners on grades 9–10 topics, texts, and issues, building on others' ideas and expressing their own clearly and persuasively.

*CCSS.ELA-Literacy.SL.9–10.5* Make strategic use of digital media (e.g., textual, graphical, audio, visual, and interactive elements) in presentations to enhance understanding of findings, reasoning, and evidence and to add interest.

*CCSS.ELA-Literacy.RL.9–10.4* Determine the meaning of words and phrases as they are used in the text, including figurative and connotative meanings; analyze the cumulative impact of specific word choices on meaning and tone (e.g., how the language evokes a sense of time and place; how it sets a formal or informal tone).

*CCSS.ELA-Literacy.W.9–10.3b* Use narrative techniques, such as dialogue, pacing, description, reflection, and multiple plot lines, to develop experiences, events, and/or characters.

*CCSS.ELA-Literacy.W.9–10.3d* Use precise words and phrases, telling details, and sensory language to convey a vivid picture of the experiences, events, setting, and/or characters.

## Essential Question

How do dialogue and authentic idioms contribute to effective storytelling?

## Objectives

| Students will understand . . . | Students will know . . . | Students will . . . |
|---|---|---|
| ■ authentic dialogue contributes to effective storytelling. | ■ idioms and slang particular to 1930s California. | ■ use idioms and slang from the 1930s to record a conversation;<br>■ understand idioms used in Steinbeck's *Of Mice and Men*. |

## Assessment Evidence

| Performance Tasks: | Self-Assessments: | Other Evidence: |
|---|---|---|
| ■ Students will work in groups to write and record a conversation. | ■ Google Forms.<br>■ Class discussion. | ■ Edmodo posts.<br>■ Students' general understanding of dialogue in *Of Mice and Men*. |

## Learning Plan

■ As an introductory activity for John Steinbeck's novella *Of Mice and Men,* students identify and define idioms from the text, work in groups to record a quick conversation using idioms from the 1930s, and reflect on how authentic dialogue can be used for effective storytelling. Previous to flipping, students were lectured about effective storytelling techniques and given a glossary of idioms to refer to while reading the novella.

**Flip:** Students use crowd sourcing and BYOD devices to create a list of idioms used and record a scripted conversation using the idioms.

■ Prior to class, students view an eight-minute video that explains and demonstrates effective storytelling techniques using dialogue. Students write up a response on a Google Form to demonstrate their understanding of the video and knowledge of effective dialogue.

■ In class, students individually scan through the text of *Of Mice and Men* and create a list of 15 slang phrases or words they find in the dialogue (10 minutes).

- As a class, students crowd source their lists by creating a master list of slang terms and phrases (7 minutes).
- Students use devices to search the Internet and define the words and phrases on the master list. It is expected that students will quickly locate a glossary of idioms listed in *Of Mice and Men* (5 minutes).
- Students divide into groups and write a one- to three-minute conversation that tells a story using the idioms from the list. The conversations will be recorded using a free MP3 voice recorder app and uploaded to Edmodo (15 minutes).
- Outside of class, students listen to the conversations and reply to each one on Edmodo explaining their opinions on and understanding of the conversation, as well as the effectiveness of storytelling through dialogue.

## Reflection Methods

- Students will do a reflective exercise (Google Form) on effective storytelling techniques.
- Students will share their thinking through discussion and Edmodo posts.

## Materials

### Facilities:

- classroom

### Equipment (non-tech):

- text for *Of Mice and Men*

### Equipment (tech):

- device to view flipped video lesson
- device to research and record idiom conversation

## Student Sample

Conversation examples can be heard at http://youtu.be/_o_ZjWFbezs.

## Reading Lesson Plan

### EXPOSITION IN *ROLL OF THUNDER, HEAR MY CRY*

*This lesson is courtesy of Ric Reyes, English teacher from Sacramento, California.*

**Topic:** Literary Analysis

**Grade Level:** 6–8

**Skill:** Identify and Analyze Structural Elements of a Story

**Established Goals:** Common Core State Standards

*CCSS.ELA-Literacy.RL.6.3* Describe how a particular story or drama's plot unfolds in a series of episodes as well as how the characters respond or change as the plot moves toward a resolution.

*CCSS.ELA-Literacy.RL.7.3* Analyze how particular elements of a story or drama interact (e.g., how setting shapes the characters or plot).

*CCSS.ELA-Literacy.RL.7.5* Analyze how a drama or poem's form or structure (e.g., soliloquy, sonnet) contributes to its meaning.

*CCSS.ELA-Literacy.RL.8.3* Analyze how particular lines of dialogue or incidents in a story or drama propel the action, reveal aspects of a character, or provoke a decision.

## Essential Question

How does the exposition of a story affect its plot?

## Objectives

| *Students will understand . . .* | *Students will know . . .* | *Students will . . .* |
|---|---|---|
| ■ a story's exposition paves the way for the plot and theme. | ■ the plot structure of stories. <br> ■ elements of exposition. | ■ analyze the impact of exposition. |

## Assessment Evidence

### Performance Tasks:

- Students will write a paragraph about how the exposition in *Roll of Thunder, Hear My Cry* affects their understanding of the plot, conflict, and characters.

### Self-Assessments:

- Class discussion and individual reflection analysis.

### Other Evidence:

- N/A

## Learning Plan

### Day 1:

**Explore:** "Prime the pump" for video content by asking students questions they can't yet answer sufficiently, thus creating a need for the flipped material.

- After reading chapter 1, ask students questions as a way of "teasing" the video. Start with basic remembering (lowest level of Bloom's Taxonomy) questions about exposition details, like "Who is our story's narrator?" to get the class comfortable with answering. I started this part as a whole class, but this can be done in small groups or as individuals with a worksheet or questions on a board or projector screen.
- Gradually move toward questions that require more inferential thinking. I ended with the question "Why is it important that we know all this information so early in the book?" For these questions, I used the Think-Pair-Share model to allow the students to rehearse their ideas before speaking them aloud to the class.
  - As they struggled to answer this question (struggle is good), I let them know I had made a video for them to watch as homework that would give them information that would help them answer this questions, and that we'd be discussing it further the next day.

At home:

**Flip:** The video is a minute and half long, and briefly covers the plot triangle, elements of exposition (setting, characters, conflict), and the significance of exposition.

- I find videos work best when students have some sort of "output," so I had them write a brief summary of the information in their Writer's Notebooks.

## Day 2:

**Apply:** I led students through guided practice with a list of questions designed to focus their attention on key details of the novel's exposition. Once they were off and running with the questions, I walked around monitoring progress and giving feedback as needed. We ended the period with a written assessment using the following prompt:

- Define exposition and explain how you see it at work in *Roll of Thunder, Hear My Cry*. Effective responses will:
    - define "exposition" clearly;
    - give two examples of exposition details in the novel, and explain how each of the two details helps set up the exposition of the novel (i.e., contributes to plot, character, or conflict).

## Reflection Methods

Again, we used Think–Pair–Share to examine what information students were missing in the Explore phase that would have kept them from being able to answer the questions in the Apply phase. Students drew conclusions about being better able to analyze the literature as a result of receiving the information in the Flip phase.

Note: I use Think-Pair-Share as a rehearsal activity for higher-level questions. After asking students a question, the room remains silent for 10–15 seconds, allowing students to begin formulating responses (Think). From there, they share and discuss responses with a partner, revising and expanding responses as they hear other ideas and perspectives (Pair). This rehearsal opportunity usually makes for greater comfort and better answers in the last step when I call on students to share with the class (Share).

## Materials

| **Facilities:** | **Equipment (non-tech):** | **Equipment (tech):** |
| --- | --- | --- |
| - classroom or computer lab | - text you are reading<br>- guiding questions for discussion | - device to view flipped video lesson (for students without home access) |

**Flipping Your Thoughts: Reflections on What You've Just Read**

In your opinion, is reading at home and discussing in class Flipped Learning?

Why do you think there is so much variety in how teachers flip reading skills?

Which of these lessons are you eager to try?

Do you have ideas for flipping reading skills that weren't covered in these lessons?

What lessons of your own do you envision flipping?

# 8

# Flipping Speaking and Listening Instruction

I was fortunate to be hired by a school that already had a culture of high expectations in the area of public speaking. However, like many teachers, I had difficulty finding time to teach these skills. Many language arts teachers struggle to work speaking and listening skills into their curriculum. This is an area in which flipping has really helped me to enhance my class by providing the time and environment to develop speaking and listening skills.

Public speaking (speeches) and live presentation are a large component of the CCSS speaking and listening skills. I've found breaking speeches down into smaller parts helps me focus on the specific needs of students. As I see it, a successful speech consists of three separate parts:

1. Writing effective language to convey the message.
2. Delivering the speech with appropriate volume, enunciation, body language, and demeanor.
3. Adding visual displays to gain interest and enhance the message.

The parts of a successful speech should initially be taught separately—because they require different skills—and then be brought together for at least one full presentation. However, my students do several presentations throughout the year, both formally and informally, to practice these different skills consistently.

# Speaking and Listening Lesson Plan

## ANALYZING FAMOUS SPEECHES

**Topic:** Speaking and Listening

**Grade Level:** 8–12

**Skill:** Identifying, Writing, and Delivering a Speech Using Effective Language Skills

**Established Goals:** Common Core State Standards

*CCSS.ELA-Literacy.CCRA.SL.2* Integrate and evaluate information presented in diverse media and formats, including visually, quantitatively, and orally.

*CCSS.ELA-Literacy.CCRA.SL.3* Evaluate a speaker's point of view, reasoning, and use of evidence and rhetoric.

*CCSS.ELA-Literacy.CCRA.SL.4* Present information, findings, and supporting evidence such that listeners can follow the line of reasoning and the organization, development, and style are appropriate to task, purpose, and audience.

*CCSS.ELA-Literacy.SL.8.4* Present claims and findings, emphasizing salient points in a focused, coherent manner with relevant evidence, sound and valid reasoning, and well-chosen details; use appropriate eye contact, adequate volume, and clear pronunciation.

*CCSS.ELA-Literacy.SL.9–10.4* Present information, findings, and supporting evidence clearly, concisely, and logically such that listeners can follow the line of reasoning and the organization, development, substance, and style are appropriate to purpose, audience, and task.

*CCSS.ELA-Literacy.SL.11–12.3* Evaluate a speaker's point of view, reasoning, and use of evidence and rhetoric, assessing the stance, premises, links among ideas, word choice, points of emphasis, and tone used.

## Essential Question

How can the use of language and oral delivery enhance the information presented?

## Objectives

| *Students will understand . . .* | *Students will know . . .* | *Students will . . .* |
|---|---|---|
| ■ a speech requires writing skills and language choices enhance a presentation. | ■ the purpose of using a variety of devices in oral presentations, including language and delivery. | ■ write and deliver effective oral presentations. |

## Assessment Evidence

| **Performance Tasks:** | **Self-Assessments:** | **Other Evidence:** |
|---|---|---|
| ■ Students will review famous speeches and analyze the effective language. | ■ Class discussion.<br>■ Reviewed presentations.<br>■ Google Forms. | ■ Students' overall speeches in the unit. |

## Learning Plan

**Flip:** Students will watch a short video (or listen to audio) of a famous well-written speech. A great resource for speeches and accompanying videos is the American Rhetoric Top 100 speeches Web site (www.americanrhetoric.com/top100speechesall.html). I usually preselect a few speeches. Review a few of your favorites and offer choices to your students. I feel offering choices gives them a little more control in the selection and they are more likely to engage in the speech or speeches they have chosen.

Students fill in Google Form identifying what language in the speech was effective.

### Day 1:

■ Begin class with a group discussion about what language the orator used in delivering his or her speech.

■ Continue the class discussion with debating how the chosen words enhanced the effectiveness of the speech.

■ Divide students into small groups based around similar speeches and hand them the printed text of the speech (or share in Google Docs).

- Each group will highlight effective passages and comment on why the group believes those passages are effective. Encourage the students to read the speech out loud as they review it, paying close attention to the language that becomes more powerful when spoken as opposed to read.
- Toward the end of the period, groups will give presentations on their selected speeches. One (or two) students will deliver two or three sections of the speeches orally, delivering them in a similar manner as the famous speakers, then one or two other students will narrate the reasons they chose those passages as being well written.

**Flip:** Students will watch a video on rhetorical devices (humor, metaphors, sonic devices). Depending on the level of your students, you could also add logos, pathos, and ethos.

## Day 2:

- Students regroup and take the speeches they previously analyzed and identify examples of rhetorical devices. Depending on the class, five is usually a good number of such devices to point out. My goal is to get students involved in discussions about the devices to facilitate their learning.
- Students then do a reflective writing exercise on what they learned about rhetorical devices.

## Extension:

This lesson should lead into another individual presentation given by the students after they have had other lessons in effective presentation skills.

## Reflection Methods

- Students will do a reflective exercise (Google Form) on the famous speeches.
- Students will share their thinking through discussion and presentations.

## Materials

| **Facilities:** | **Equipment (non-tech):** | **Equipment (tech):** |
|---|---|---|
| - classroom | - If devices are not readily available, print out text of speeches. | - device to view flipped video lesson |

# Speaking and Listening Lesson Plan

## BAD POWERPOINTS

**Topic:** Speaking and Listening

**Grade Level:** 8–12

**Skill:** Identifying and Producing Effective Visuals for a Presentation

**Established Goals:** Common Core State Standards

*CCSS.ELA-Literacy.CCRA.SL.2* Integrate and evaluate information presented in diverse media and formats, including visually, quantitatively, and orally.

*CCSS.ELA-Literacy.CCRA.SL.5* Make strategic use of digital media and visual displays of data to express information and enhance understanding of presentations.

*CCSS.ELA-Literacy.SL.8.5* Integrate multimedia and visual displays into presentations to clarify information, strengthen claims and evidence, and add interest.

*CCSS.ELA-Literacy.SL.9–10.5* Make strategic use of digital media (e.g., textual, graphical, audio, visual, and interactive elements) in presentations to enhance understanding of findings, reasoning, and evidence and to add interest.

*CCSS.ELA-Literacy.SL.11–12.5* Make strategic use of digital media (e.g., textual, graphical, audio, visual, and interactive elements) in presentations to enhance understanding of findings, reasoning, and evidence and to add interest.

## Essential Question

What digital media tools enhance presentations effectively?

## Objectives

| *Students will understand . . .* | *Students will know . . .* | *Students will . . .* |
| --- | --- | --- |
| ■ visuals are important for enhancing a presentation. | ■ the available digital media that can be added to presentations. | ■ identify effective digital media to enhance presentations. |

## Assessment Evidence

| **Performance Tasks:** | **Self-Assessments:** | **Other Evidence:** |
| --- | --- | --- |
| ■ Students will review and make poorly designed presentations.<br>■ Students will finish the lesson with a well-designed presentation. | ■ Class discussion.<br>■ Reviewed presentations.<br>■ Google Forms. | ■ Students' reactions during presentations. |

## Learning Plan

**Flip:** Students will watch a short video of a really bad visual presentation. There are many to be found on YouTube or you can make your own. There is one by stand up comedian Don McMillan that is very funny (http://youtu.be/KbSP-PFYxx3o). The goal is for the visual displays to be blatantly bad.

Students fill in Google Form identifying what elements in the video were poor presentation visuals.

### Day 1:

- Begin class with a group discussion concerning why the different visuals were poor.
- Continue the class discussion on how the visuals could have been better.
- Divide students into small groups.
- Each group will receive a set of four slides with text only and be asked to make them unattractive and poorly designed.
- Toward the end of the period, students will present their slides to the class, pointing out the poor choices they made.

**Flip:** Students will watch one or two videos of short, visually appealing presentations. TedTalk videos (http://www.youtube.com/user/TEDtalksDirector) has some good ones if you want to find one or make your own.

## Day 2:

- Start class with a group discussion on identifying effective visuals.
- Students will go back into groups and redesign their slide presentations.
- Toward the end of the period, students will present their slides to the class, pointing out the reasons they believe the visuals they chose are effective.

## Extension:

This lesson should lead into another individual presentation given by the students after they have had lessons in effective oral presentation skills.

Note: Tools that I like for creating visually attractive presentations include Haiku Deck (www.haikudeck.com) and SlideRocket (www.sliderocket.com). Google Slides is also a good resource.

## Reflection Methods

- Students will do a reflective exercise (Google Form) on good and bad presentation visuals.
- Students will share their thinking through discussion and presentations.

## Materials

| **Facilities:** | **Equipment (non-tech):** | **Equipment (tech):** |
|---|---|---|
| - classroom | - If devices are not readily available, print out slides and students can use colored pencils to enhance them visually. | - device to view flipped video lesson |

# Speaking and Listening Lesson Plan

## WHERE DO MY HANDS GO?

**Topic:** Speaking and Listening

**Grade Level:** 5–12

**Skill:** Delivering a Speech Using Effective Oral Delivery Skills

**Established Goals:** Common Core State Standards

*CCSS.ELA-Literacy.CCRA.SL.4* Present information, findings, and supporting evidence such that listeners can follow the line of reasoning and the organization, development, and style are appropriate to task, purpose, and audience.

*CCSS.ELA-Literacy.CCRA.SL.6* Adapt speech to a variety of contexts and communicative tasks, demonstrating command of formal English when indicated or appropriate.

*CCSS.ELA-Literacy.SL.5.4* Report on a topic or text or present an opinion, sequencing ideas logically and using appropriate facts and relevant, descriptive details to support main ideas or themes; speak clearly at an understandable pace.

*CCSS.ELA-Literacy.SL.6.4* Present claims and findings, sequencing ideas logically and using pertinent descriptions, facts, and details to accentuate main ideas or themes; use appropriate eye contact, adequate volume, and clear pronunciation.

*CCSS.ELA-Literacy.SL.7.4* Present claims and findings, emphasizing salient points in a focused, coherent manner with pertinent descriptions, facts, details, and examples; use appropriate eye contact, adequate volume, and clear pronunciation.

*CCSS.ELA-Literacy.SL.8.4* Present claims and findings, emphasizing salient points in a focused, coherent manner with relevant evidence, sound valid reasoning, and well-chosen details; use appropriate eye contact, adequate volume, and clear pronunciation.

*CCSS.ELA-Literacy.SL.9–10.6* Adapt speech to a variety of contexts and tasks, demonstrating command of formal English when indicated or appropriate.

*CCSS.ELA-Literacy.SL.11–12.6* Adapt speech to a variety of contexts and tasks, demonstrating a command of formal English when indicated or appropriate.

## Essential Question

How can a speaker's demeanor (eye contact, speaking voice, hand gestures) enhance a speech's effectiveness?

## Objectives

| *Students will understand . . .* | *Students will know . . .* | *Students will . . .* |
|---|---|---|
| ■ a speaker's demeanor plays a role in the speech's effectiveness. | ■ the elements necessary for effective presentations (hand gestures, eye contact, etc.). | ■ write and deliver effective oral presentations. |

## Assessment Evidence

| **Performance Tasks:** | **Self-Assessments:** | **Other Evidence:** |
|---|---|---|
| ■ Students will review a well-delivered and a poorly delivered speech given by a peer (if possible). | ■ Class discussion.<br>■ Reviewed presentations.<br>■ Google Forms. | ■ Students' overall speeches in the unit. |

## Learning Plan

**Flip:** Students will watch two short videos of student-delivered speeches. One is an excellent example. One is an average or maybe slightly above average example (you have to be careful with this one because the students should understand what their speeches will be used for). I use speeches given by previous students (with their permission) who are no longer at the school to avoid social issues at school.

Students fill in Google Form comparing the delivery of each student.

**Day 1:**

■ Begin class with a group discussion comparing the two speakers. This, along with the Google Forms, should give you as the teacher an idea of what the class already understands about effective speaking skills and where the students need help.

- If you have theater students in your school or excellent improv speakers, have them visit the class and give a cold read of a speech focusing on delivery and not content. There's something about a live delivery that is more effective than a video performance. I always have a few students whom I've worked with previously and who have this ability to be given any text and turn it into a great speech. If you don't have them, skip this step. (Another resource to consider is a drama teacher or other dynamic teacher.)
- Students should pair off and be given a short text of a prewritten speech.
- After about 10 minutes of prep time, students deliver the speech to their partners.
- The partners will informally critique the speech givers' technique, focusing on body language, eye contact, and volume, not speech content or fluidity (considering the short preparation time).
- Toward the end of the period, have another group discussion about what the critics looked for, what was difficult for the speakers, and what skills need improvement.

**Flip:** Students will watch a video on what students should be aware of when delivering a speech. Things like volume, enunciation, hand gestures, posture, and eye contact are all important. I have included a sample of my rubric for oral delivery of a speech that I use.

## Day 2:

- Students group with another partner and are given the text of a speech.
- After a preset preparation period, students deliver the speeches to each other, again receiving critiques.
- With the remaining time and on Day 3 (if necessary), students should give their speeches to the entire class. Use your discretion as to whether to have every student do this exercise or not. Keep in mind that the best way to improve speaking ability is practice. If students struggle to deliver in front of a larger audience, the best way to practice is in front of a larger audience.

## Extension:

This lesson should lead into another individual presentation given by the students after they have had other lessons in effective presentation skills.

## Reflection Methods

- Students will do a reflective exercise (Google Form) on the example speeches.
- Students will share their thinking through discussion and presentations.

## Materials

### Facilities:

- classroom

### Equipment (non-tech):

- If devices are not readily available, print out text of speeches.

### Equipment (tech):

- device to view flipped video lesson

# Rubric Sample

*Delivery* (100 points)  Area to Improve  Area of Strength

---

**Appearance:**  0  2  4  6  8  10
Did the student appear confident, well-dressed, and comfortable, smile, and make eye contact with everyone?

---

**Eye Contact:**  0  2  4  6  8  10
Did the student distribute eye contact equally with the entire audience?

| | |
|---|---|
| Looked at notes too much | Seldom had to look at notes |
| Focused only on certain people | Looked around the entire room |
| Needed to look at the extreme sides | Looked at the people on |
| of the room | the extremes! |

---

**Posture:**  0  2  4  6  8  10
Did the student stand up straight and keep weight balanced evenly on both feet without locking knees?

| | |
|---|---|
| Swaying, leaning to one side | Stood up straight! |

---

**Gestures:**  0  2  4  6  8  10
Did the student use effective gestures that were big and above the waist?

| | |
|---|---|
| Clasped hands together or behind back | Very natural gesturing |
| Played with fingers or jewelry | Definite, energetic gesturing |
| Held an arm, crossed arms | Able to keep hands relaxed to |
| | sides when not gesturing |

---

**Facial**                  0     2     4     6     8    10
**Expressions:** Did the student use appropriate, animated facial expressions?

Smile!                         Great smile!

---

**Volume:**           0     2     4     6     8    10
Did the student use appropriate volume so everyone in the room could easily hear?

Louder!                        Easily heard

---

**Articulation:**      0     2     4     6     8    10
Did the student use clear articulation and pronounce words correctly?

| | |
|---|---|
| Dropping "g" off "ing" words | Hit word endings nicely |
| Articulate word endings to prevent running words together | No slurring |
| Refrained from using "ummm" or "like" to fill pauses | All words pronounced correctly |

---

**Vocal**                  0     2     4     6     8    10
**Expression:** Did the student use variety in rate, pitch, and volume and have good vocal quality?

---

**Composure:**      0     2     4     6     8    10
Did the student appear confident by displaying fluency, vocal confidence, and controlled body?

| | |
|---|---|
| Vocalized pauses | No vocalized pauses! |
| Fidgeting with hair, clothing, jewelry, fingers | Looked very relaxed |
| Stepping around nervously | Looked in control |
| Breathe deep! | Great breathing |

---

**Energy and Enthusiasm:**  0     2     4     6     8    10
Did the student present a positive energy?

Energize!                     Wow!

_____ **Score**

# Speaking and Listening Lesson Plan

## SOCRATIC SEMINAR

*Public speaking is not the only skill that falls under speaking and listening. The ability to collaboratively discuss with others is also a skill. Here is another lesson provided by Kate Baker, high school English teacher from Manahawkin, New Jersey.*

**Topic:** Speaking and Listening Skills

**Grade Level:** 9–10

**Skill:** Discussing Concepts from Novel Study

**Established Goals:** Common Core State Standards

*CCSS.ELA-Literacy.SL.9–10.1* Initiate and participate effectively in a range of collaborative discussions (one on one, in groups, and teacher led) with diverse partners on grades 9–10 topics, texts, and issues, building on others' ideas and expressing their own clearly and persuasively.

*CCSS.ELA-Literacy.SL.9–10.1a* Come to discussions prepared, having read and researched material under study; explicitly draw on that preparation by referring to evidence from texts and other research on the topic or issue to stimulate a thoughtful, well-reasoned exchange of ideas.

*CCSS.ELA-Literacy.SL.9–10.1c* Propel conversations by posing and responding to questions that relate the current discussion to broader themes or larger ideas; actively incorporate others into the discussion; and clarify, verify, or challenge ideas and conclusions.

*CCSS.ELA-Literacy.SL.9–10.1d* Respond thoughtfully to diverse perspectives, summarize points of agreement and disagreement, and, when warranted, qualify or justify their own views and understanding and make new connections in light of the evidence and reasoning presented.

*CCSS.ELA-Literacy.SL.9–10.3* Evaluate a speaker's point of view, reasoning, and use of evidence and rhetoric, identifying any fallacious reasoning or exaggerated or distorted evidence.

*CCSS.ELA-Literacy.SL.9–10.4* Present information, findings, and supporting evidence clearly, concisely, and logically such that listeners can follow the line of reasoning and the organization, development, substance, and style are appropriate to purpose, audience, and task.

*CCSS.ELA-Literacy.SL.9–10.5* Make strategic use of digital media (e.g., textual, graphical, audio, visual, and interactive elements) in presentations to enhance understanding of findings, reasoning, and evidence and to add interest.

## Essential Question

How can students share, support, prove, and refute ideas in a class discussion?

## Objectives

| *Students will understand . . .* | *Students will know . . .* | *Students will . . .* |
|---|---|---|
| ■ that in-depth knowledge of a topic is needed to engage in an academic discussion. | ■ how to engage in an academic Socratic seminar. | ■ engage in an informed Socratic discussion;<br>■ use a rubric to evaluate a peer's performance;<br>■ evaluate their evaluator. |

## Assessment Evidence

| **Performance Tasks:** | **Self-Assessments:** | **Other Evidence:** |
|---|---|---|
| ■ Students will choose a role (see my handout at http://tinyurl.com/mvjz8lh) and participate accordingly in the Socratic discussion. | ■ Google Form reflection. | ■ Edmodo posts. Peer assessment via rubric (http://tinyurl.com/mg4a8ln).<br>■ TodaysMeet archive. |

## Learning Plan

■ As a culminating activity for novel study, students prepare, engage, and assess each other in a Socratic seminar.

**Flip:** Students will demonstrate higher-level thinking skills by preparing, participating, and evaluating each other in a Socratic seminar rather than taking a test on a subject.

- Prior to class, students organize notes and prepare possible answers to suggested discussion topics.
- In class, students choose a role in the discussion, sit in an appropriate position, and sign on to TodaysMeet.com.
  - 30 students = 10 students in the inner circle and 20 students in the outer circle (http://tinyurl.com/mvjz8lh).
- The inner circle will answer questions aloud in a verbal discussion.
  - During the first half of the period, five students will speak while five shadow the speakers.
  - Switch midway through the period so that the shadowers become the speakers.
  - Shadowers complete a rubric assessing the speakers (http://tinyurl.com/mrnghdz).
- Outer circle will listen and respond in a back channel chat on TodaysMeet.com.
  - During the first half of the period, 10 students will actively chat in the back channel while the other 10 shadow the chatters.
  - Switch midway through the period so that the shadowers become the chatters.
  - Shadowers complete a rubric assessing the chatters (http://tinyurl.com/mrnghdz).
- In the case of odd numbers, assign the unpaired student to be the moderator of the discussion. He/she monitors the backchannel and asks the speakers questions from the chatters, as well as moves on to a new discussion topic.

The teacher projects the directions on the front board. An example from our Socratic seminar on *West Side Story* and *Pygmalion* can be found here: http://tinyurl.com/l6p2kp5.

- Either the teacher or the moderator projects one question at a time and keeps the conversation flowing while monitoring the back channel discussion for comments and questions from the outer circle.
- When time is called, the circles switch to give the shadowers a chance to engage in the conversation.

At the end of the period, students give their rubric to the person they shadowed. The active participant then reviews the rubric and completes a Google Form reflection on the conversation and evaluation. Students also publicly share their thoughts in their small groups on Edmodo.

## Reflection Methods

- Students will do a reflective exercise (Google Form) on effective discussion techniques.
- Students will share their thinking through discussion and Edmodo posts.
- Students will review peer-assessed rubrics on their performance in the discussion (evaluating how well they were evaluated).

## Materials

### Facilities:

- classroom
- desks arranged with 5 desks in inner circle and 25 desks in outer circle

### Equipment (non-tech):

- list of possible discussion questions
- copies of the text
- student notes

### Equipment (tech):

- netbooks, chromebooks, or laptops
- TodaysMeet.com

## Student Sample

Blog post with example of backchannel from the Steinbeck Socratic Seminar: http://kbakerbyodlit.blogspot.com/2012/10/like-shooting-fish-in-barrel-structured.html

## Flipping Your Thoughts: Reflections on What You've Just Read

How can speaking and listening skills be enhanced by flipping lessons?

Which of these lessons are you eager to try?

Prior to CCSS, did you do many lessons focusing on public speaking?

What lessons of your own do you envision flipping?

# Other Uses for Flipping Language Arts

One of the most exciting parts of Flipped Learning for me was the options that opened up for me because of the flip. I was able to get more creative with projects, to encourage more collaboration between students, deliver more lasting feedback, and even help students create content themselves.

## Student Feedback

One-on-one conferencing with students is extremely beneficial for students—I enjoy having the time in a Flipped Classroom to have conversations with students every day about their work. However, at times, students may forget what you said to them in class. Or they may have feedback from you written on their paper (or commented in Google Docs) and don't quite understand it when reviewed later. To help with this, I give audio and video feedback regularly, in addition to the conference or sometimes even simultaneously.

For this, I've used a variety of multimedia tools to deliver that feedback. Initially, I was screencasting their Google Docs and recording my audio explaining comments as I typed them into the paper. The video screencast could then be e-mailed to the student. That process wasn't bad, but took longer than I liked and, therefore, wasn't really sustainable long term. I'm all about being efficient with my work (without sacrificing student improvement), because that is more likely to be effective. Some of you may find this solution perfect for your situation.

Next, I began using a whiteboard app on the iPad. I chose Explain Everything because it had the most versatility for what I wanted to accomplish. There are other free apps, like Educreations or ScreenChomp, but I preferred Explain Everything. I would import the students' documents to the "whiteboard" then use a stylus pen and write my feedback on the document while also recording my audio explaining what I was marking. The students then got a video of my feedback on their document. This method was more efficient for me. I did like this method and still use it, but was concerned about my comments not living with the document. If a student wanted to review those comments without my audio, they could not with reviewing the video again.

I knew teachers who were using recorded audio from Google Voice and placing the link into the document and I had considered trying that method. Then came VoiceComments for Google Drive. It is a Chrome extension that can be added to your Internet browser and that works in conjunction with Google Drive and Google Docs. I go through the document first and type any comments or comment shortcuts that I want. Then, I simply open the document in VoiceComments (directly from Google Drive) and record my audio while viewing the document. After I'm finished, I click "share" and the link to the audio comment is placed into the document alongside my typed comments.

With Explain Everything and VoiceComments, I would also at times record my writing conference with a student, including the questions they asked, and then send them that link after class. That way, the student could re-listen to the conversation we had as many times as he or she needed.

These aren't the only methods of giving audio/video feedback. These are just the ones that worked for me. As technology changes, our ability to give audio feedback is only going to improve. It's exciting to think of the options available to benefit our students with detailed multimedia feedback.

## Peer Feedback

Peer feedback can be very helpful or not depending on the student giving the feedback or the process. As a teacher, I really wanted my students to help each other improve their writing. As I mentioned earlier, I wanted to create a community of writers. I knew how vital it was for my own writing to get multiple viewpoints and revisions. But I struggled to get my students to embrace that process.

I'm aware peer feedback has been around for years and many teachers use it in their non-flipped ELA classes quite effectively. For me, it wasn't until I flipped and created the in-class environment where students felt invested in each other that was I able to get the most out of peer feedback. Now, students can have productive conversations with each other in class. I can also facilitate peer-to-peer discussion about work and help guide the discussion to being more effective. Students see the value of what their peers have to say because I'm available to answer questions, guide discussions, and model appropriate feedback in class with them.

I've also enhanced the peer feedback process by adding technology to the process. Originally, I used Google Forms for the students to enter their feedback on another student's work. Then, I would review the feedback and forward it to the other student. Over time and collaboration with Kate Baker on ways to use scripts with Google Forms, we came up with a way to use a mail merge script with the peer feedback process (Baker, 2013).

The peer feedback I get from my students since flipping my class has proven profoundly beneficial in not only improving their writing, but also creating that community feeling in my class I so desired before.

## Student-Created Content

I believe, as do many, that the value in technology is not in simply consuming content, but actually creating content. If we put a tablet or laptop in students' hands and expect them only to read books electronically or take "interactive" tests, then we are missing the true value of having these devices and losing valuable learning opportunities for our students. That being said, some creation tools took so much instruction from me to get the students proficient enough to create that I felt I was teaching the technology more than I was teaching the content I wanted the students to gain. The dissonance and frustration created by struggles with the device could often inhibit student learning. I found this technology to still be important, but needed ways to give my students more support.

In 2011, I met Eric Marcos, the creator of Mathtrain.tv. Marcos's students had been making math instruction videos for several years and he realized that power and created his site to distribute those videos (Marcos, 2012). In a moment of inspiration, I decided to create a language arts site of a similar nature and launched Engliteo.com.

Now, students in my class create ELA content videos and I use some of the better ones on this Web site. Since I flipped my classroom, I have the time to support students in the video creation process. I also know and have experimented with multiple ways to make videos and can guide the students to the best way for them based on available devices and resources.

In addition to having the inquiry learning happening while they create their videos, I also have a database of videos that other students in my class or around the world can use to aid their own learning.

## Creative Projects

Do you have creative project ideas for your class and just can't find the time to implement them? I did as well. Some of my more exciting projects became possible because I had the time available in my Flipped Classroom. I always did fun experiments with my students in class before flipping. I had a *Lord of the Flies* survival simulation, a *The Outsiders* mock trial, a Scrooge for mayor (*A Christmas Carol*) campaign project, and more.

I had a small two-week project I called the Choose Your Own Project that I did toward the end of the school year with my eighth graders that they looked forward to all year. I loved the creative ideas and the enthusiasm they put into these projects, but didn't have the time to expand the timeline. I read about Google 20% Time and an idea called "Genius Hour" in *Drive* by Daniel Pink (2009). In the book, Pink talks about the policy that Google employees are allowed 20% of their work week to focus on a project of interest to them *not* related to their job. This concept, not started by Google, is responsible for many Google products that many people use today. The idea is if you give employees autonomy, encourage them to improve or master something of their interest, and give them a purpose in what they do, your employees will be happier and more productive in the long run. With flipping my class, I was now able to take a two-week Choose Your Own Project and expand it over the entire year, renaming it the 20% Time Project.

This book isn't about my 20% project, so I won't go into detail here about the logistics of it. If you want more information, my colleague Kate Petty created a Web site at www.20timeineducation.com that serves as a wonderful resource for teachers.

Another exciting project I was able to improve on because of flipping was my Anne Frank Museum. Prior to flipping, the Anne Frank Museum was displayed in our school gym, science fair style, and students and parents would walk through and admire the displays relating to Anne Frank. The problems I had with the project were that the students had to work mostly at home, the displays (although usually well designed) weren't technologically advanced (most consisted of a poster board of some sort), and other students had to take time from class to view the exhibits. Since flipping, I was able to have the students assemble a digital Anne Frank Museum online. Their exhibits could be worked on entirely in class and therefore the inquiry happening while they were researching and designing their project was happening with me present to give guidance. A recent version of the museum can be seen at http://goo.gl/x6IgR.

Those are just a few of the ideas available to me since I flipped my class. Because the spirit of the Flipped Classroom is innovation, there is no limit to the amount of creative ideas you can add to your classroom.

## Flipping Your Thoughts: Reflections on What You've Just Read

Do you have great project ideas that you've never had time for before?

Do your students embrace that sense of community needed for effective peer feedback?

Have you struggled in the past to give your students time for quality peer feedback?

Have you struggled in the past to find time to give your students feedback?

Have you spent hours making comments on paper only to have them thrown in the recycle bin on the way out the door?

# Tips for Making Engaging Videos

We can't all be Bill Nye the Science Guy. He has a team of writers, a director, cameramen, and editors to help him create his videos. If you're like me, you don't have that. I had to make a lot of videos before I figured out some key elements to help make the videos more engaging and increase the likelihood the students will watch them all the way through. Based on my own trial and error and discussions I've had with other flippers, I came up with a list of 13 tips to help you make better videos.

## High Energy (I Mean Over-the-Top Energy)

Many people don't realize that your demeanor and personality seem very muted when put on video. Just as an actor will tell you, you need to overact in order to appear normal. I don't know the science behind this (I mean, I'm an English teacher), but—trust me—it's true. So, if you just have a normal conversation with the camera, it will come across as dull and possibly even as though you're bored. When you create the video, you need to ramp up your energy to uncomfortable levels and when played back it will appear closer to normal.

A good way to practice this is to record yourself having a normal conversation where you are explaining something. Maybe talk to your spouse, your friend, or your dog. Play that video back and see how engaging you come across. Next, ramp up your energy as much as possible, use your hands to gesture (even if you aren't on camera), really play to the camera. Re-watch that and see if you sound and look more engaging. Continue this exercise until you've found an energy level that really hooks the audience.

After you've found the energy level, you need to find a way to tap into it consistently and sustain it. Admittedly, there are times when I'll turn to caffeine to boost my energy. You'll need to find a way to give yourself a boost on those days when you're tired or distracted, but need to get a video recorded. For me to sustain that energy, I would make four or five videos in one sitting. I would prepare my visuals in advance and then sit down at one time and knock out several videos. With this process, I could produce four or five videos in an hour and I could also sustain my energy level throughout the process.

## Student Reflection

Many people forget this key piece of the process. You should add pieces of reflection to the videos that will make the students think about what it is that they've just watched. If we expect the students to just view the video and nothing else, you won't find much value in the videos. There needs to be a reflection piece. I use a combination of note taking and Google Forms. I'm not a big fan of asking students to pause the video, do an exercise, then unpause to continue watching. The reason I don't like that method is that you are asking the students to delay gratification (finishing the video) and asking them to do an exercise that won't get immediate feedback for them. Which is going to have more pull? My guess would be finishing the video.

I ask students to take notes during the video answering certain questions along the way. I do a note-taking lesson early in the year to teach the students effective note taking. When I do a note check in class, I ask deeper questions to see if they can process the information and use it in a different context. This helps me assess understanding. If a student's notes are incomplete (or in some cases too complete), poorly organized, or not effective, I can give him or her individualized instruction on how to improve the notes.

Like a lot of other flippers, I also use Google Forms. I create a Google Form asking key questions I want them to answer after the video to show their thinking process. I'll embed the video and Google Form together on a Google site or blog so students have them in one place. After watching the video, they fill in their answers and click "submit." I then get a spreadsheet of all the students' answers and can review and assess them. Many teachers use this process to determine what topics to focus on in class. It also gives me an easy way to see who is watching the video.

If a paper form or guided notes is more your preference, Crystal Kirch has an excellent form she uses for her flipped math classes that she calls WSQ (pronounced "wisk"). WSQ is an acronym for Watch-Summarize-Question. She uses the WSQ forms in much the same way others use a Google Form (Kirch, 2012). Even though Kirch is a math teacher, the WSQ form concept can be modified to fit your class.

Whatever you find works best for your class, it is important to make sure to add a reflection piece to your videos.

## Script or No Script? That Is the Question.

Some people have a dynamic speaking ability and can turn on the camera and the words just seem to flow. I don't. I even do improv comedy as a hobby where the point is to think on your feet and entertain and I can't do it with my videos. Most people, I believe, don't have that ability. In that case, a script or outline is best. I recommend starting with a script. It does take a little longer to prep for a video if you write out a script, but it will help you get a sense of timing and make sure you don't forget anything. Once you start to get a feel for the flow needed from scripting, you can move to working from outlines. I have a habit of saying "um" when I'm thinking. Therefore, I need to leave myself little time to think while I am recording a video. Obviously, you know your personality and presentation style better than I do, but I think it is critical for the overwhelming majority of teachers to work from an outline at a minimum. We teach our students the importance of prewriting. We should practice that too.

## Keep It Short

When some people first hear about Flipped Learning, they envision students watching videos more than 20 minutes long. I don't think it is any surprise that students won't watch videos this long. A good rule of thumb is one minute per grade level as a maximum time. So an 11th grader's videos should only be 11 minutes long as a maximum. Now, I can't always keep my videos to the maximum amount of time for my classes (which would be seven or eight minutes), but because the majority of my videos fall in the four to seven minute range, my students know I do respect their time and try to keep the videos short.

Students' attention span is limited even with the most engaging content. Find ways to keep your content concise and efficient. If your video is getting significantly longer than it should be and you feel you can't cut anything, make it a two-part video and have the students watch it over two or three days.

You also have to consider that the time on the video isn't always the viewing time. It can take your average student about twice as long to watch a video with pauses as the actual run time. So a five-minute video will take most of your students 10 minutes or more to watch. Early in the year, I ask my students to keep track of how much time they are spending watching the videos. If I find a student is spending an hour on a seven-minute video, I need to fix that. Either the student is too meticulous with trying to process every detail of the video, or the information is too complex for him or her to understand. In either case, that is an opportunity for me to individualize my instruction for that student. I've told the too-meticulous student to cut watching the videos off at 20 minutes. I've told the struggling student to try and gain smaller concepts or I give him or her tips of what to watch for in the videos. Sometimes it requires me to sit and watch a video with students individually and walk them through the thought process involved. But the flexibility of a Flipped Classroom allows me to do that.

At first, your videos will be longer than needed. That's another reason an outline is good. But it is imperative for the long-term success of a Flipped Classroom to keep the videos short. The length of your videos can adversely affect the quality of your instruction. My goal is always a video under five minutes. Sometimes I make it, sometimes I don't. But my students appreciate and have more buy-in knowing that I try.

## Personalize

Flipped Learning is all about developing better relationships with your students. Personalizing your videos is a big step in developing those relationships. I recommend teachers make the majority of their own videos. It is alright to supplement on occasion with other teachers' videos, but shouldn't be the norm for your class. Students want to see their teacher even if your video is not as good as someone else's. They want to hear your voice and feel like you are talking directly to them. I also put on screen shots of me in nearly every video I make. Not the entire time, but at least the intro and outro. Some free screencasting programs won't allow you to put your webcam image into the video. If possible, find a way to make that happen. It seems small, but it really makes a huge difference for the students.

## Tell Stories

Going along with personalizing and building relationships, it is important to tell personal stories that relate to the content. I hope we all know what is too personal to share, but recounting some life lessons really draws in your students. Sharing some of your interests, just as you would in the classroom, makes the students see you as human. A great storyteller can weave a lesson throughout a story but keep students on their seats until the end. It may not be a good idea to start with sharing stories in your videos if that isn't something you've done in the past, but experiment with it. Tell some non-embarrassing stories to introduce a topic and set up an expectation or to conclude a topic to really hit home an idea.

## Create with Another Teacher

When I began flipping, I searched for another English teacher willing to make videos with me and was unsuccessful. I forged on anyway and made all my videos solo. And you can do that. But, in their book, *Flip Your Classroom,* Bergmann and Sams say, "There is something powerful about watching two people have a conversation instead of watching one teacher talk at the viewer" (Bergmann & Sams, 2012). I absolutely agree. The dynamic of having someone to play off of in your videos makes them infinitely more interesting. Additionally, having someone to share the workload can reduce the amount of stress and anxiety new flippers may feel. If you cannot find someone in your own district or town, reach out to others online. I can't think of a better way to model collaboration for your students than for them to see you collaborating with another teacher in your videos.

## Make It Multimodal

Have you ever been in a class where the teacher instructs the same way every day? Did you like that class? If that teaching style worked for you, then you may have. However, most prefer some variety. The same is true for videos. You should add more to your videos when possible. In other words, make the videos multimodal.

Images can elicit an emotion response, either positive or negative. Add images to your visuals to create connections. Haiku Deck is an excellent resource for Creative Common stunning presentation-ready images. Add clips of video from others or movies to hit home a message you're trying to convey. I have former students make videos as a "guest speaker" and I package my own content sparingly around their videos. This variety in style, voice, and presentation really adds punch to your videos. However, don't forget to keep your videos copyright friendly. Once your videos are out in the public realm, you never know who might stumble across them.

## Go on Location

It is always great to see how excited students can be on field trips. There is just something special about seeing an occurrence happen that makes it more real. Therefore, I suggest you go "on location" for as many videos as you can. It is easier for science teachers to get video of observable scientific phenomenon for their videos. But ELA teachers can get creative. I saw an artistic bench at the Indianapolis Museum of Art that reminded me of the Freytag Pyramid of plot structure. So I went back with my video camera and recorded footage of me on the bench. When I visited Monroeville, Alabama on vacation, I recorded me saying a few words outside the *To Kill a Mockingbird* museum. English and reading does happen in the real world. Get creative in finding ways to link an image, a background, a setting to the content and it becomes more tangible for the students. You don't have to record the whole video on location. Sometimes I'll observe something that I think would be great. Rather than write my whole video right then, I'll record some video with my smartphone or video camera to use as an introduction. If you see a humorous sign with a grammar error, take a picture to show your students. Some of you may teach in schools where your students rarely get to travel outside of your town. With technology today, it is now easier than ever to bring that world to them. I can assure you, my students cannot go to the Indianapolis Museum of Art now without thinking of plot structure.

## Consider Interactivity

"One of the criticisms of this teaching tool [the Flipped Classroom] is that students receive knowledge in a passive state—by watching video," says Jac de Haan (2011). We've addressed that criticism in one way by adding a student reflection piece. It can also be addressed by adding interactivity. Admittedly, this takes some technical skills and may not be for everyone. But having students interact with the video by clicking answers or actively directing parts of the video can be very powerful in engaging students in the content. Camtasia Studios has a robust array of interactive features for quizzing, tables of contents, and more to add to your videos. YouTube has annotation features that can be added simply. Once you get down an efficient video-making process, I encourage you to experiment with different methods of interactivity to take your videos to the next level.

## Done Is Better Than Perfect

Jon Bergmann often says when he presents, when determining the right time to finish a video, a good rule of thumb is, "Do you need it perfect or do you need it Tuesday?" Many flippers early on in their video-making process spend way too much time trying to make the videos perfect. Kevin Brookhouser turned me on to this concept of "done is better than perfect" that he got from Facebook. The idea is that trying to be perfect prevents you from getting other things done. There are times when perfection doesn't matter and it only prevents you from being finished (Brookhouser, 2012). As long as there are no major issues with the content of the video, don't worry so much about making mistakes. If you're like me, you make mistakes in your classroom. Why shouldn't you allow yourself to make them on video? Put in some sloppy transitions every now and again, stumble over your words, briefly forget you're recording and talk to someone else in the room. All experienced flippers have made these mistakes and more. Adopt the philosophy that "done is better than perfect" and move on. Besides, you need that video by Tuesday!

## Use Self-Reflection

Many teachers have a fear of being on camera. They are nervous about putting their videos out there where others might see them. That is a natural fear, but one you must get over. A good exercise to do is to make a handful of videos first. Then show them to a small audience of trusted friends and family. Get their honest feedback. Then reach out to experienced flippers and see if they have the time to critique one of your videos. Get their honest feedback. If you have the time, get a few trusted children (maybe your own kids or the neighbor's kids) of similar age to your students and ask them to watch a video or two. Get their honest feedback. Once you've gone through this process, you should have a good deal of information on what could be better in your videos. Self-reflecting on this feedback will not only improve your videos, it will improve your teaching.

If you are afraid when recording the videos, you will come across as timid and unsure. Find someone to give you a pep talk or do it yourself. If you show confidence and bravery, think of the example you are showing your students. I once heard someone say after viewing some bad teacher videos, "Whether you like these videos or not, you have to admit it takes courage to put your work out there for everyone to critique." Most of my videos are in public spaces, like YouTube. Many get thousands of views from people I have no idea who they are. It could be a student from another school trying to learn the topic. It could be a teacher from another school looking to flip. It could be a parent wanting to see what his or her child is learning. All of them probably have some opinion about my methods and ability as a teacher based solely on the video. I can't worry about that. My priority is the students in my classroom. My videos are made for them. Others are free to privately enjoy, critique, or gain material from my videos. So possibly my biggest advice is to put those doubts and fears out of your mind and just do it. You'll be glad you did.

## Have Fun

I can't stress this one enough. Maybe I should have put it first instead of last. Have fun! You're embarking on a journey that is going to transform the way you teach. Enjoy the process. Let students see you having fun making your videos. Tell jokes. Laugh at yourself. If you're having fun, and showing it, it's more likely your students will have fun. I remember one video I did on different types of verbs. Every time I said "intensive verbs" I did my best Hulk Hogan impression. (For those under 30, Hulk Hogan was a popular professional wrestler in the '80s. Google him.) "That is an INTENSIVE verb!" I would proclaim. I was having fun and my students had fun right along with me when they watched the video. Those moments still happen in the classroom even if they were started on video. It's that relationship thing again. Are you sensing a theme? Flipped Classrooms are about creating better relationships with your students. Why wouldn't you have fun doing that?

## Flipping Your Thoughts: Reflections on What You've Just Read

What are some fears you have about making videos?

Do you have ideas for how to add a reflection piece to your videos?

Are you willing to take constructive criticism early on to improve your videos?

Can you give yourself permission to have fun during this whole process?

# 11

# FAQs and Resources

As I do presentations and training across the country, many of the same questions tend to come up. You may have asked many of those questions while you were reading this book. This chapter is designed to answer many of the most common questions and provide resources that can get you started on the path to flipping.

## How Long Should the Videos Be?

I know I mentioned this in a previous chapter, but I wanted to reiterate it for those who may have flipped directly to this section. They should be short! The rule of thumb I use is that the maximum should be one minute per grade level. A 10th grade student shouldn't have videos more than 10 minutes. An 8th grader shouldn't have videos longer than 8 minutes. Remember, that is the *maximum* length. Most should be shorter than that. If you can't get the information in under that time, you're trying to get too much across in the video. I will admit occasionally (maybe twice a school year) I will go over the recommended maximum length. However, I've developed a relationship with my students in which they are willing to watch a longer video or two because they know that isn't the norm. Really challenge yourself to keep your videos short. It will go a long way in helping your Flipped Classroom succeed.

## What Do You Do about Students Without Access?

In 2011, 75% of households reported having a computer and 71% reported having Internet access (U.S. Census Bureau, 2013). Despite these statistics, many teachers have some (or maybe most) students without reliable Internet access at home. However, that shouldn't be an impediment to flipping your class. Some methods that I've seen to be successful:

- **Offer before- or after-school time.** Open up your classroom or a computer lab for 30 minutes before or after school. Students should be able to watch their videos in the 30 minutes. It does take motivation on the students' part to come in early or stay late. However, if you offer that consistently and the students choose not to come, there is a bigger issue to deal with outside of simply having access.

- **Use flash drives.** For students who have a computer, but not good Internet access, put your videos on a loaner flash drive. Students can transfer the files to their own flash drive to take home or you can loan out your flash drives, depending on your situation. I also knew of a teacher who used a grant to buy a handful of small video players that could be loaned out to students.

- **Use smartphones or iPods.** A number of students, especially high school students, have smartphones that are video capable. If you make your videos smartphone friendly, some could watch them that way. Some of my students actually prefer to watch the videos on their smaller screen devices. One of the reasons I like using YouTube is that it is device agnostic and thus it doesn't require you to make multiple versions of your videos to work across several devices. This option is popular with students who may have a long commute to school or take the team bus to a week-night sporting event. They can make productive use of that time by watching videos.

- **Use DVDs.** You would be hard pressed in today's society to find a student who doesn't have access to a DVD player. Many of the current game systems even play DVDs. Your videos can be burned to DVDs and distributed to those students. It takes a little extra work and organization on your part, but because it is to support student learning, it is well worth it. If you come across a student who truly doesn't have a DVD player, DVD players can be picked up at many resale stores, like Goodwill, for $20. Or maybe another parent would be willing to donate their old DVD player to a student in need.

- **Watch in class.** One criticism of the Flipped Classroom is that it is reliant on homework. Some teachers and administrators argue against giving home-work at all. I don't require my students to watch the videos outside of class. Many of my students still choose to watch them at home for whatever reason, but they don't have to. I have some students who have the ability to come into class, watch the necessary video, and still participate in any activities or complete the in-class work. If a student cannot manage that process, then an individual conversation is had to determine if it is the best method for that student. Some teachers may not agree with this method. I just want to put as few impediments in the way of my students' learning as possible. And, if allowing them to watch some of their videos in class helps, then I'm willing to do it. Now, here is a caveat to this: I don't tell them that at the beginning of the year. (To my future students: if you just read this, forget you read that.) Some students would hear that and get in their mind they can watch all their videos in class and there is no reason to come prepared. I believe how you present that choice is important to its effectiveness. There should be expectations of necessary elements for a student to succeed in your class. One of mine is coming to class prepared to work. If students understand that, then I'm fine with giving them the choice to watch a video during class.

## What Do You Do With Students Who Don't Do the Homework?

Some teachers say, "Well, my students don't do homework now, how will I get them to watch the videos?" and "What do you do when they don't watch the videos?" Here's the truth of the matter: students who consistently don't complete assignments aren't going to miraculously begin watching your videos. So, what steps do you have in your class now to ensure students turn in assignments? This argument also operates under the assumption that students who don't watch the videos would have listened to the content if it was delivered in class as direct instruction. How often is that the case? Here are the steps that I, and other teachers, take regarding students who don't watch videos:

- **Watch in class.** As I mentioned in my answer to the last question, I just have them watch in class. The great thing about a Flipped Classroom is that I can talk to my students every day. When I find a student hasn't watched the video, I'll say, "Fine, watch it now and I'll be back to discuss when you're finished." Some students legitimately forget. Some may be too busy that night. Some may have watched it, but had too many distractions going on and didn't retain any information. I don't immediately begin reteaching material if the student hasn't first invested the time to try to understand the video. I get to know my students well enough over the year to tell who watched the video and is struggling to understand the material and who didn't watch the video and is trying to get me to believe they did. Sometimes, the student may miss out on an in-class activity because they are catching up on the video. And, with a Flipped Classroom, you don't have to repeat direct instruction because it is on video.

- **Give alternatives to video.** Some students may not learn well from video. Because you can talk to every student in class, this is an excellent opportunity to discuss with the students how they believe they learn best. I've actually had a student ask if she could take the textbook home and read it because the videos didn't work for her. Seriously! If the student is truly motivated to learn, you shouldn't have too much trouble finding a method that works for the student and for you. If the student is a reluctant learner, then you need to address his or her motivation issues and not the video issue. Some students find the videos may actually be easier than their other options and will start watching them. With the flip, you have the time to have those conversations.

- **Use small-group direct instruction.** Some teachers have their classes arranged so that they have an area designated to direct instruction. Students who need the lesson, whether because they didn't watch the video or they watched it but struggled to understand, sit in that area and the teacher gives a quick lesson on the topic. I see this mostly in math classes. If you go this route, you should monitor the numbers who are using this time to avoid having to watch the videos. This should also not become a full-blown lesson. If you're doing this for too long, you aren't able to give your other students the attention they need, thus negating the point of a Flipped Classroom. I recommend this only as a last option if other methods didn't work.

I would add that if a lot of students aren't watching the videos, you need to resolve the bigger issue at hand. The video is rarely the problem (unless it's too long). This is where your expertise as a teacher comes into play. Find the reasons students aren't watching the video and address those.

## I'm Sold on Flipping, But I Have No Idea How to Make the Video. What Tools are Available for Creating Videos?

There are a number of tools out there, both free and paid, that can make videos. It all depends on your situation, technical ability, and outcome goals.

- **Camtasia Studio by TechSmith.** This is the most popular screencaster ($299 PC, $99 Mac). This program has the most features you'll find, including multiple-layer tracks, graphics, copyright-free music and animations, quizzing options, and more. Its comprehensiveness can be overwhelming to some at first. The cost can also be too much for some if you are still experimenting with flipping. One "secret" is that if you go to a workshop sponsored by TechSmith, you get the software discounted. TechSmith is really committed to helping educators and it shows in its products. Most teachers I know who have been flipping for an extended period of time eventually upgrade to Camtasia Studio.
- **Screencast-o-matic** (www.screencast-o-matic.com). This is a free online screencasting tool. It is a simple tool for those just getting started. It does have certain limitations. It doesn't allow you to record to your webcam and it limits you to 15 minutes. They do have a yearly plan ($15/yr) that addresses some of the limitations of the free version. I have not tried it, but hear good things from those on a limited budget. It also requires java, so it is not available on some devices.
- **CamStudio** (http://camstudio.org). This is a free, open source download, not to be confused with Camtasia Studio. I have no experience with this product, but it is free, so may be worth a try.

- **Google+ Hangout.** An often overlooked feature of Google+ Hangout is the ability to screen share. Simply record a live Hangout and screen share your content. This only records to YouTube and you would have to download and edit in another application. But I use it frequently for quick videos I need to make and the content is automatically on YouTube, so there is no need for me to spend time uploading.

If you use an iPad:

- **Explain Everything** (www.explaineverything.com, $2.99). This is an interactive whiteboard app and screencaster that will record images, text, video, and writing on your iPad while you narrate. For my uses, I've found it to be the most versatile in not only its input options, but also its output options. You are free to output your video to several options and that's what got me willing to pay for the app.
- **Educreations** (www.educreations.com, free) This is an interactive whiteboard app, but it is also an Internet app. It does many of the same things Explain Everything does. The difference I've found is that it only allows output to the Educreations Web site. However, some teachers embed the video on their Web site to make it easier for the students to find.

A handful more screencasting options are available with a Google search. These are just a few I've had experience with or know teachers who have used them as a viable option in their classrooms. Test the ones that sound best to you and find what works best for your classroom.

## OK, I've Made Some Videos, Now Where do I Put them So the Students Can See?

A valid question for many. Flipping your class is very difficult if the students can't find your videos. Actually, it's impossible. As with screencasting tools, I'll list a few that I'm familiar with and you can try different methods that work for your class.

- **YouTube** (www.youtube.com) So, who hasn't heard of YouTube? I can assure you your students have. The largest user group of YouTube is teens. I like You-Tube because the videos can be played on any device. The process to upload, organize, and manage your videos is easy. You have access to those videos, but don't need to take up hard drive space storing them. You can keep private videos private, limit access by making videos unlisted, or throw them up for public view. However, if you go this route, I recommend you turn off commenting and rating features. This is a distraction that students don't need. I realize, in some schools, YouTube is blocked. Whatever the reasons, I would ask your administration if that could be unblocked, or you could try YouTube EDU. If that isn't an option, then you need to look elsewhere. Regardless, I would still upload your videos to YouTube to keep an archive of them for yourself.

- **Screencast.com by TechSmith** (www.screencast.com, free limited version, or $99.95/yr). This is an option provided by TechSmith if you want a place to store your videos. It can be a bit costly if you need a lot of space, which most flippers do. However, one great feature is that the interactivity features (like quizzes) in Camtasia Studio are optimized to work on Screencaster.com. It allows you a clean space to upload and organize your videos. It also gives you some analytics features that can be valuable.

- **TeacherTube** (www.teachertube.com). This is an education-friendly Web site designed for teachers to upload videos for free. The site allows video reviews and is checked for appropriate content. This can be an option for you if YouTube is blocked in your school. The interface isn't as intuitive as YouTube, but is a good option if YouTube is not.

- **Google Drive** (drive.google.com). If you teach at a Google Apps™ for Education school, this is another option available to you. Videos can be uploaded to your Google Drive account and then shared with your students (or placed in a shared folder). The downside to this is that Google only allows 15GB of free storage and that could be eaten up pretty quickly by uploading a lot of videos. If you have a smaller collection of videos or don't mind deleting videos from your Google Drive as it fills up, this is an option for you.

## How Do You Get Administrators' Support?

As any good politician will say, "Know your constituents." I was fortunate to have supportive and trusting administrators that allowed me the freedom to make this work. I know other teachers who aren't so fortunate. First, I would recommend you do your research. Reading this book is a start. You should also consider attending a workshop, reading blogs, and watching webinars. Show your administrators you are really focused on doing this right. Try to anticipate their questions and reach out to experienced flippers for answers. One major key to a successful Flipped Classroom is flexibility. Be willing to be flexible in how you implement flipping in your class.

A lot of administrators ask for research. Admittedly, the research on Flipped Learning specifically is limited. I've given some of the research in this book. More research is in process now. The Flipped Learning Network is a good resource for a collection of current research.

I also encourage you to invite an open door to your classroom once you flip. Anyone walking into my classroom would see students who are engaged, collaborating, and actively learning, and a teacher giving individual attention to several students. Transparency in practice and open classroom visits can be a very powerful defense of the Flipped Classroom.

## How Do You Get Parents' Support?

Again, I've been fortunate in this area. I've had a lot of positive response from parents. Many of the same points for getting administrators' support can be used for getting parents' support. Meeting with parents to discuss their concerns is helpful. Again, transparency in practice and having an open classroom goes a long way in creating positive dialogue with parents. It is a good idea to direct parents to resources you've come across like YouTube videos or blog posts.

I recommend explaining to parents exactly what your class will look like when you begin flipping. Just as you now have time in class to have positive discussions with your students, take the time to have similar discussions with parents. Stress the flexibility to make adjustments, the individualization of your instruction, and the support you can give every student. It's hard to be against that.

## What Are Some Excellent Resources?

- **Flipped Learning Network** (www.flippedlearning.org). The Flipped Learning Network was founded by Aaron Sams and Jon Bergmann in 2012. It does an excellent job of providing workshops and webinars on Flipped Learning. Sams and Bergmann also collect news and research related to Flipped Learning.
- **Flipped Learning Ning** (www.flippedclassroom.org). The Flipped Learning Ning was started by Jerry Overmyer as a social network of flipped teachers looking to connect with other flipped teachers. It hosts a lot of groups specific to content areas and age groups. There are moderators for each group with the intention of keeping the information current.
- **Cycles of Learning** (www.cyclesoflearning.com). This is a blog and resource site put together by Ramsey Musallam. It is an excellent way to learn more about the Explore-Flip-Apply model and how inquiry can be further developed in a Flipped Classroom.
- **Turn to your Neighbor: The Official Peer Instruction Blog** (http://blog.peerinstruction.net/). This blog is maintained by Julie Schell and has a lot of great information about peer instruction.
- **Flipped Learning Network Podcast** (www.edreach.us/channel/flipped-learning). This is my weekly podcast in which I interview teachers around the world to discuss Flipped Learning. If you have a long daily commute or like to listen to podcasts when you exercise, download the podcast and listen.

**Flipping Your Thoughts: Reflections on What You've Just Read**

Where can you go to get questions answered I may not have covered here?

Do you feel confident enough in the answers to your questions to begin your flip?

Where will you direct others with similar questions?

Is flipping right for you?

# Conclusion

If you've made the decision to flip your English class, you may be the only one in your school doing so. I found it a lonely journey at times. However, reaching out to the Flipped Learning community through the Ning and Twitter gave me a lot of support. Many of the early flippers who were once just names on a blog post are now friends. Not only do they share and problem solve with me, they also challenge me to reflect on my practices. Although some may call me an expert in flipping, I don't presume to have all the answers. I am modifying my class all the time to find what's best for my students. It is difficult for me to sum up what Flipped Learning has meant to me. And that is because it is still changing; it is still improving.

Flipping isn't the answer to change education and none of the Flipped Learning leaders have said that. However, it can be a piece of the puzzle. It can be a bridge to better teaching, to better job satisfaction, and to better learning. I know, prior to flipping, I was on the verge of leaving education. Now, I see so much potential in what can be accomplished that I can't imagine not being part of this. This has been my story—the lessons I've learned. I can make no guarantees as to where your journey will take you. But, no matter what path you choose, you will be a better teacher for it.

# References

Anderson, J. (2005). *Mechanically Inclined: Building Grammar, Usage, and Style into Writer's Workshop.* Portland, ME: Stenhouse.

Atwell, N. (1998). *In the Middle: New Understandings about Writing, Reading, and Learning.* Portsmouth, NH: Boynton/Cook.

Baker, K. (2013, April 6). Writing about Grading (Again) [Web log post]. Retrieved from http://kbakerbyodlit.blogspot.com/2013/04/writing-about-grading-writing-again.html

Baker, W. (2000, April 15). "The 'Classroom Flip': Using Web Course Management Tools to Become the Guide by the Side." Edited by Jack A. Chambers. *Selected Papers from the 11th International Conference on College Teaching and Learning* (Jacksonville, Florida, April 12–15, 2000).

Bennett, B. (2011, October 18). Video is Not the Answer [Web log post]. Retrieved from http://www.brianbennett.org/blog/video-is-not-the-answer/

Bergmann, J. (2012, December 18). Flipped Learning #26: The Power of the Transformation with Jon Bergmann [Audio blog interview by T. Cockrum]. Retrieved from http://edreach.us/podcast/flipped-learning-26-the-power-of-the-transformation-with-jon-bergmann/

Bergmann, J., & Sams, A. (2012). *Flip Your Classroom: Reach Every Student in Every Class Every Day.* Eugene, OR: International Society for Technology in Education.

Brookhouser, K. (2012, August 4). A Letter to My Students and Parents about the 20% Project [Web log post]. Retrieved from http://www.iteachithink.com/2012/08/a-letter-to-my-students-and-parents.html

Burgess, D. (2012). *Teach Like a Pirate: Increase Student Engagement, Boost Your Creativity, and Transform Your Life as an Educator.* San Diego, CA: Dave Burgess Consulting.

Calkins, L. (1986). *The Art of Teaching Writing.* Portsmouth, NH: Heinemann.

ClassroomWindow and Flipped Learning Network. (2012). *Flipped Classrooms: Improved Test Scores and Teacher Satisfaction.* Retrieved from http://classroomwindow.com/flipped-classrooms-improved-test-scores-and-teacher\satisfaction

Council of Writing Program Administrators, National Council of Teachers of English, and National Writing Project. (2011, January). *Framework for Success in Postsecondary Writing.* Retrieved from http://wpacouncil.org/framework

De Haan, J. (2011, September 26). Interactive Flipped Instruction with YouTube™ Annotations and Time-Markers [Web log post]. Retrieved from http://www.techwithintent.com/2011/09/interactive-flipped-instruction-with-YouTube/

Driscoll, T. (2012). *Flipped Learning and Democratic Education* (Unpublished master's thesis). Columbia University. Retrieved from https://docs.google.com/file/d/0B0VIwE5hKSWta0RqbmdZSGh0WTQ

Graham, S., & Perin, D. (2007). *Writing Next: Effective Strategies to Improve Writing of Adolescents in Middle and High Schools. A Report to Carnegie Corporation of New York.* (Rep.). Retrieved from http://carnegie.org/fileadmin/Media/Publications/PDF/writingnext.pdf

Green, G. (2012, July). *The Flipped Classroom and School Approach: Clintondale High School.* Lecture presented at Annual Building Learning Communities Education Conference, Boston, MA. Retrieved from http://2012.blcconference.com/documents/flipped-classroom-school-approach.pdf

Hicks, T. (2009). *The Digital Writing Workshop.* Portsmouth, NH: Heinemann.

Hicks, T. (2013). *Crafting Digital Writing: Composing Texts across Media and Genres.* Portsmouth, NH: Heinemann.

Hicks, T., Hunt, B., & Kajder, S. (2010). *Creating Opportunities for Learning with Newer Literacies and Technologies: Three Reports from Cyberspace.* Paper presented at National Council of Teachers of English (NCTE) National Conference, Orlando, FL.

Khan, Sal. (2011). "Let's use video to re-invent education." *TED: Ideas Worth Spreading.* http://www.ted.com/talks/salman_khan_let_s_use_video_to_reinvent_education.html

Kirch, C. (2012, March 31). Submitting the WSQ Online via Google Forms [Web log post]. Retrieved from http://flippingwithkirch.blogspot.com/2012/03/submitting-wsq-online-via-google-forms.html

Marcos, E. (2012, September 12). Eric Marcos: Students Use Tablets for Math Video Tutorials Comments. Education Week. Retrieved from http://www.educationnews.org/technology/eric-marcos-students-use-tablets-for-math-video-tutorials/

Mazur, E. (1997). *Peer Instruction: A User's Manual.* Upper Saddle River, NJ: Prentice Hall.

Moran, C., & Young, C. A. (In press). "Active Learning in the Flipped English Language Arts Classroom." In J. Keengwe, G. Onchwari, & J. Oigara (Eds.), *Promoting Active Learning through the Flipped Classroom Model.* Hershey, PA: IGI Global.

Musallam, R. (2011, September 26). Explore-Flip-Apply: Introduction and Example 1 [Web log post]. Retrieved from http://www.flipteaching.com/files/0e82357541a89a8888c1a7c498c1c201–4.php

Musallam, R., & Highfill, L. (2013, June 19). Flipped Learning #47: Live from #FlipCon13 with Ramsey Musallam [Audio blog interview by T. Cockrum].

Retrieved from http://edreach.us/podcast/flipped-learning-47-live-from -flipcon13-with-ramsey-musallam/

Pink, D. (2009). *Drive: The Surprising Truth About What Motivated Us.* New York: Riverhead Books.

Pink, D. (2010, September 12). "Think Tank: Flip-Thinking—The New Buzz Word Sweeping the US." *The Telegraph.* Retrieved from http://www.telegraph .co.uk/finance/7996379/Daniel-Pinks-Think-Tank-Flip-thinking-the-new -buzz-word-sweeping-the-US.html

Project Tomorrow. (2013). 2013 Trends in Online Learning: Virtual, Blended, and Flipped Classrooms. Retrieved from http://images.email.blackboard.com/ Web/BlackboardInc/%7B829dd21f-b3f2–409e-9a34-e37de5835c74%7D _k12Trends2013_web.pdf

Schell, J. (2013, March 11). Use of the Term Flipped Classroom [Web log post]. Retrieved from http://blog.peerinstruction.net/use-of-the-term-flipped -classroom/

Schneider, B., Wallace, J., Blikstein, P., & Pea, R. (2013). "Preparing for Future Learning with a Tangible User Interface: The Case of Neuroscience." *IEEE Transactions on Learning Technologies, 6*(2), April-June 2013, 117–129. Retrieved from http://www.computer.org/cms/Computer.org/transactions/tlt/pdfs/ tlt2013020117.pdf

Strayer, J. (2007). *The Effects of the Classroom Flip on the Learning Environment: A Comparison of Learning Activity in a Traditional Classroom and a Flip Classroom that Used an Intelligent Tutoring System* (Unpublished doctoral dissertation). Ohio State University. Retrieved from http://etd.ohiolink.edu/view.cgi/Strayer%20 Jeremy.pdf?osu1189523914

Tenneson, M., & McGlasson, R. (2005, November 5). *The Classroom Flip: Presentation on Using Technology in Blended Classrooms to Free up More Class Time for Active Discussion.* Lecture presented in Springfield, MO, Missouri Teaching and Learning Mentoring Project Best Practices Conference.

Thompson, M. C. (2013) *Word Within the Word.* Unionville, NY: Royal Fireworks Press.

Truss, L. (2003). *Eats, Shoots & Leaves.* New York: Gotham Books.

U.S. Census Bureau (2013). *Computer and Internet Use in the United States.* Retrieved from http://www.census.gov/prod/2013pubs/p20-569.pdf

Zellner, A., & Beauchamp-Hicks, S. (2009). *Using Google in Ways That Haven't Even Been Invented Yet: Visionary Reports from Cyberspace.* Paper presented at the NCTE Conference, Orlando, FL.